CHILDREN OF POVERTY

STUDIES ON THE EFFECTS OF SINGLE PARENTHOOD, THE FEMINIZATION OF POVERTY, AND HOMELESSNESS

edited by
STUART BRUCHEY
ALLAN NEVINS PROFESSOR EMERITUS
COLUMBIA UNIVERSITY

A GARLAND SERIES

Neighborhood Context and the Development of African American Children

M. Loreto Martinez

GARLAND PUBLISHING, INC.
NEW YORK & LONDON

Published in 2000 by
Garland Publishing, Inc.
A member of the Taylor & Francis Group
29 West 35th Street
New York, NY 10001

Garland is an imprint of the Taylor & Francis Group

10 9 8 7 6 5 4 3 2 1

Library of Congress Cataloging-in-Publication Data is available from the Library of Congress.

ISBN 0-8153-3538-5

Printed on acid-free, 250 year-life paper
Maufactured in the United States of America

To my family

Contents

Acknowledgments

Support for this research was provided by the Bureau of Maternal and Child Health Grant # MCJ-240621, and the National Center on Child Abuse and Neglect Grants # 90CA1401 and 90CA1621.

Tables

Figures

NEIGHBORHOOD CONTEXT AND THE DEVELOPMENT OF AFRICAN AMERICAN CHILDREN

CHAPTER 1

The Role of Neighborhood Characteristics in Child Development

The evidence of worsening life conditions, concentration of poverty (Jargowsky & Bane, 1991; Pandey & Coulton, 1994; Wilson, 1991) and high degree of African American segregation in urban areas (Gephart, 1989; Jencks & Mayer, 1990; Massey & Denton, 1989; Wacquant & Wilson, 1993) has led to a growing interest in how neighborhood contexts effect child development and parenting behavior (Coulton, Korbin, & Su, 1996; Coulton, Korbin, Su, & Chow, 1995). Further, changes observed during the last three decades in the socioeconomic composition and patterns of racial segregation of the neighborhoods in which low-income children and their families reside have added a sense of urgency to understanding the nature of neighborhood effects (Anderson, 1991; Brooks-Gunn, Duncan, Klebanov, & Sealand, 1993; Jencks & Mayer, 1990; Jencks & Peterson, 1991; McLanahan & Garfinkel, 1993).

Central to the current study is the question of how contexts often labeled as disadvantageous—such as inner-city neighborhoods in which many African American families reside—influence the development of preschool children. From a theoretical perspective, both the ecological (Bronfenbrenner, 1979) and transactional (Sameroff & Seifer, 1995) approaches to the study of human development have acknowledged the importance of community factors in shaping child development. Neighborhoods are part of the environments in which children live, specifically, part of the exosystem that affects children's current and future development, and are sources of both stressors and resources (Horowitz, 1989; Sandler, 1985).

Implicit in the ecological conceptualization of human development is the assumption that neighborhood characteristics engender a social context which influences the individual perceptions and attitudes that ultimately guide the behavior of parents. Specifically, that neighborhood characteristics operate indirectly through the more proximal determinants of child development, such as parental perceptions of resources available, family social interaction, and parental competence. However, from an empirical point of view questions about how neighborhood context influences development remain unanswered.

To date it is unclear how neighborhood characteristics influence development. Direct effects of neighborhood quality could involve an actual deprivation of opportunities and resources that make certain experiences possible for children. For example, inner-city neighborhoods may offer an impoverished array of experiences and opportunities for children and families residing in them. Findings from a study by Gaster (1993) suggest that increasing crime, traffic, and deterioration of parks and playgrounds have cut off children and youths from safely using their neighborhood resources.

Or, neighborhood characteristics may influence child development by affecting the extra-familial environment (i.e., threat of crime, lack of support). For example the extra-familial environment for families living in poor, inner-city neighborhoods is by no means benign and supportive. Garbarino and Sherman (1980) contend that some neighborhoods work for parents and children while others work against them. Areas are considered "low-risk" if they help support families and overcome a family's internal weaknesses, and "high-risk" if they compound internal family problems. Consequently, high-risk neighborhoods are not good places to bring up chil-

se a family's own problems may be compounded
ameliorated by the neighborhood context.

tively, actual neighborhood characteristics could
velopment through characteristics of the neigh-
the level of its social networks and organizations.
study contributes to our understanding of these
pirically exploring pathways by which neighbor-
may be related to child development

veral processes that can be assumed to intervene
g neighborhood influences on development, the
will examine the role of parenting. A contextual assumes that parents and children are not pas-
sive recipients of neighborhood influences but actively interact with their neighborhood environment. Studies that have
examined the determinants of success among children growing up in poverty confirm that some parents are able to mar-
shal their efforts and some not (Furstenberg, 1993; Jarrett,
1995). Consequently, we can not assume that a given neighborhood will have the same effects on every child, regardless
of his/her family background. Therefore, elaborating on the
need to examine how children and parents organize, adapt to,
and shape their immediate environments (Bronfenbrenner,
1986), the current study will explore the role of parenting style
as a mediator of neighborhood influences on development.

The following questions will be addressed: Are neighborhood characteristics associated with the developmental outcome of African American preschool children? If so, which
neighborhood characteristics—objective or perceived—contribute the most to the variance in child development at age
five? Do perceived neighborhood characteristics make a
unique contribution to children's development beyond that of
structural characteristics of neighborhood? Are these effects
independent, or is there a mediational effect at age five? Are
perceived neighborhood characteristics associated with children's development because they affect the abilities of parents
to parent? If so, are perceived neighborhood characteristics

associated with parenting style? Are the effects of perceived neighborhood mediated by parenting style?

In addition to the ecological perspective, two other theoretical developments inform the current study:

1. Environmentalists and community psychologists have identified physical and social dimensions of neighborhoods that are important determinants of individual behavior. Particular emphasis is given to reviewing findings regarding the social component of neighborhood life (e.g., formal and informal social exchanges, emotional, instrumental, and informational support because it appears to play a central role in terms of providing resources for coping with stressors both at the individual and neighborhood level, and has been linked to positive child rearing (Cochran, 1988; Cochran & Brassard, 1979). This literature is reviewed as a framework for the development of a measure of parental perceptions of neighborhood, the Perceived Neighborhood Scale (PNS).

2. Social organization theory (Sampson, 1992) is used as a theoretical framework to examine the relationships between structural ratings (e.g., poverty, unemployment, residential mobility, vacant housing) and maternal perceptions (e.g., embeddedness in social networks, satisfaction with neighborhood, sense of community, threat of crime) of the neighborhood context and the developmental outcome of preschool children.

To summarize, from an ecological perspective, early child development occurs within the multiple contexts of the home, the school, the neighborhood, and other social units. The aim of this study is to understand development in context by focusing on the role of neighborhood influences early in child development. Findings are expected to shed light on the pathways by which family (i.e., maternal perceptions of neighborhood threats and resources) and community resources (i.e., objective ratings of neighborhood) influence development.

The book is organized in five chapters. This first chapter introduces the questions to be addressed and the purpose of the study. The second chapter provides a framework for studying neighborhood influences in context and a theoretical background for the development of the Perceived Neighborhood Scale. The third chapter describes the methods for the study. The fourth chapter presents the results of the study. Finally, the fifth chapter discusses the findings and addresses the limitations of the study.

CHAPTER 2

Neighborhood Context and Child Development

FINDINGS AND LIMITATIONS OF AVAILABLE STUDIES

There has been a recent increase in the number of studies with an explicit focus on neighborhood dynamics, particularly on the neighborhood networks in which individuals and families are embedded, and the implications of these relationships for child and family well-being (Bursik & Grasmick, 1993; Kupersmidt, Griesler, De Rosier, Patterson, & Davies, 1995).

Evidence supporting the influences of neighborhood characteristics on child development comes from different sources. For example, studies have found that child maltreatment is a symptom of neighborhood and community trouble (Garbarino & Kostelny, 1992; Garbarino & Sherman, 1980) and suggest that concentrated neighborhood poverty (Drake & Pandey, 1996), community disorganization (Coulton, Korbin, Su, & Chow , 1995) and lack of social coherence characterize areas with the highest risk of maltreatment

In a replication of Garbarino and Sherman's (1980) study, Deccio, Horner, and Wilson (1994) found a strong relationship between neighborhood economic levels and incidence of child maltreatment. Their results also indicated differences in other neighborhood characteristics: (a) families in their low-maltreatment neighborhoods were more likely to have lived in the neighborhood for more than five years, and to have a telephone, and (b) there were fewer vacant housing units in low-risk neighborhoods. These findings of community-level correlates are consistent with those reported by Zuravin (1989), who found that the strongest predictors of maltreatment rates were low income and rate of vacant housing, and suggest that other features of the neighborhood such as the availability of resources, and the attachment to neighborhood are associated with children's development.

Similar findings are reported from a recent study of the ecology of maltreatment rates in urban neighborhoods in Cleveland. Coulton et al. (1995) examined the relationship between structural characteristics of the neighborhood (i.e., economic status, population movement, age, family structure and proximity to other areas of poverty concentration) and maltreatment rates in 177 residential census tracts. Three factors— impoverishment (poverty rate, unemployment, vacant housing, population loss, female- headed families and percentage of black population), child care burden (amount of adult supervision and resources that may be available for children), and instability (degree to which the area may be characterized by movement of residents) plus a measure of geographical location explained almost half the variance among census tracts in their child maltreatment rates. The impoverishment factor had the greatest effect on maltreatment rates. Interestingly, the macro-structural factors related to community social organization displayed similar explanatory power with respect to violent crime, drug trafficking, juvenile delinquency and teen childbearing.

Overall, the above reviewed studies provide cross-sectional evidence of the possible influences that neighborhood social conditions have on children's well-being. By focusing on the community itself, these studies have identified neighborhood conditions that place children at risk. However, caution in generalizing from their findings is warranted since these studies have not controlled for the selection effects that bring certain families into particular neighborhoods.

Although recent years have witnessed a rapid increase in the number of studies examining neighborhood effects on individuals and families, few studies have paid attention to the effects that changes in the ecology of neighborhoods may have on parenting behavior and the developmental outcomes of young African American children. Most studies have focused on adolescence (Brewster, 1994; Sampson & Laub, 1994) and explored the main effects of neighborhood characteristics on a certain outcome or status at a single point in time. For example, using data from the Neighborhood Characteristics Files of the 1970 Census, Crane (1989;1991) found sharp increases in school dropout probabilities and teenage childbearing for both African American and whites living in very bad neighborhoods, particularly in urban ghettos. Other quantitative research has examined the relationships between socioeconomic composition and racial mix of schools and neighborhoods on a range of outcomes for individuals (Jencks & Mayer, 1990). Another line of research has examined the association between neighborhood environment and fertility-related behaviors among African American adolescents (Brewster, 1994; Brooks-Gunn, Duncan, Klebanov, & Sealand, 1993; Hogan & Kitagawa, 1985). In brief, few studies have addressed the question of how neighborhoods shape development and these have been focused on adolescents; even fewer have examined the processes by which neighborhoods influence development in young children.

With a few exceptions (Brooks-Gunn et al.,1993), research on the effects that neighborhoods have on child development has been hampered by the lack of longitudinal data and by the absence of studies combining information at the individual, family, and neighborhood level (Brooks-Gunn et al., 1993; Furstenberg & Hughes, 1994). The latter is probably due to several factors such as the fact that methods for measuring the neighborhood context have been limited (Coulton et al., 1996;

Kupersmidt et al.,1995), empirical measures of neighborhood effects are still underdeveloped, and theoretical issues regarding neighborhood conceptualizations are far from elaborated (Burton, Price- Spratlen & Spencer, 1997; Wilson, 1996). Further, efforts to model the effects of neighborhoods on parents and children have been constrained by the lack of suitable measures of neighborhood environments that are pertinent to parents and young children. The current study will address the limitations of former studies by including neighborhood variables at the individual, family, and aggregate level, and from different sources. Additionally, the study will contribute by developing a measure of perceived neighborhood context that is suitable for parents.

STUDYING NEIGHBORHOOD INFLUENCES IN CONTEXT

A contextual approach assumes that child development is determined not simply by a single factor, but more by the interplay among child, family, and environmental characteristics (Sameroff & Seifer, 1995). For example, to understand the processes by which disadvantaged neighborhoods place children at risk for poor cognitive and socio-emotional development, it is important to identify protective and risk factors for development operating at different levels of the social context (i.e., individual, family, community) (Sameroff & Seifer, 1995). Findings from available studies that have taken a contextual approach (Brooks-Gunn, 1996; Brooks-Gunn et al.,1993; Ensminger, Lamkin, & Jacobson, 1996; Kupersmidt et al., 1995) suggest that the intersections between individuals, families, and their environments need to be examined in order to understand how micro environmental and macro environmental influences interact to shape development.

Most studies done to date ask simply whether there is a neighborhood effect on children's outcome; few focus on the types of effects observed. An exception is the study by Brooks-Gunn et al. (1993) that used two data sets that included information at all three levels (i.e., individual, family, and neighborhood) to elucidate ways in which residence in low-income and affluent neighborhoods affected the cognitive and behavioral development of children. Examining how neighborhood and family characteristics were related to outcome in early childhood and late adolescence, findings indicated powerful neighborhood effects—particularly the presence of affluent neighbors—on children's IQ, teenage births, and school dropout, after differences in the socioeconomic characteristics of families were adjusted for. To summarize, children growing up in affluent neighborhoods did better developmentally than children in low-income neighborhoods, an effect that persisted even when family-level differences were controlled.

Findings from another recent study provide support for the importance of exploring the interactions between family and neighborhood contexts. Examining childhood aggression in the context of family and neighborhood factors, Kupersmidt et al. (1995) found a main effect for family type (i.e., single versus two-parent households). However, the main effect for family type was qualified by a significant Family Type X Neighborhood Type interaction. Although low-income African American children living in single-parent homes were the most aggressive, this finding was true only for those who were also living in a low-SES neighborhood. Therefore, support for the hypothesis that the neighborhood context is associated with childhood aggression and peer relations over and above the variance accounted for by family characteristics was provided.

From the findings of Kupersmidt et al. (1995) it can be inferred that neighborhoods and families do not have uniform roles in how they may relate to aggression and peer adjustment in childhood. Each of these contextual factors can have a positive, negative, or neutral influence on development, depending on the domain of children's functioning under investigation. At the family level, it can be assumed that parents who invest in their children by establishing and maintaining obligations may be more apt to create opportunities and safer niches for their children. Parents' ability to create and sustain a normative system in the household and to generate reciprocal obligations with their children can be thought of as family-based social capital (Coleman, 1988). The latter interpretation is consistent with theoretical views about the complex nature of the relation between ecological factors and individual behavior.

Because neighborhood life encompasses phenomena at different levels of analysis, identification of neighborhood characteristics and neighboring behaviors that enhance child well-being should be based on a contextual assessment (Brooks-Gunn, 1996) in which individual, family, community and societal factors are considered. This context includes family members and relatives as well as the nature of the neighborhood (i.e., who lives there, the physical arrangements that exist, the daily hassles and crises that affect social interactions, and political and economic factors related to these events).

A contextual perspective to investigate the influences of neighborhood characteristics on child development adds further complexity because it can be assumed that neighborhood influences represent a subtle and changing blend of social and individual processes. Thus, the effects are likely to be indirect, with their impact depending upon the interaction of neighborhood characteristics with each other, as well as with those of families, households, social networks, and individuals.

The rationale presented above provides the basis for the development of a multilevel model to conceptualize the influences of neighborhood characteristics on the development of urban African American children. The ecological perspective assumes that neighborhood characteristics engender a social context which influences the individual perceptions and attitudes that ultimately guide the behavior of parents. More specifically, neighborhood—as reflected in structural ratings of the area—can be seen as an exogenous influence that operates indirectly through the more proximal determinants of child development, such as parental perceptions of resources available, family social interaction, and parental competence.

For the current study, it is hypothesized that the effects of structural characteristics of the neighborhood on children's development at age five are mediated by parental perceptions of neighborhood characteristics. The issue of how perceptions of threats and resources available in the neighborhood might be related to children's development and through which processes (e.g., parenting) will also be addressed. Developmental outcomes will be examined in two domains— cognitive and social development— at two points in time (i.e., child age three and age five).

THE SOCIAL ECOLOGY OF POOR NEIGHBORHOODS

Neighborhood Poverty

Poverty contributes to the social and economic decline of urban neighborhoods and is associated with higher rates of teenage pregnancy, delinquency, crime, drug related problems, and declining housing values (Coulton & Pandey, 1992; Massey & Denton, 1989). The harshness of living in a poor neighborhood is only partly economic (i.e., residents of poor neighborhoods are more often victims and perpetrators of crime, they are more likely to have problems with substance abuse, more likely to be victims of racial discrimination, and are exposed to more environmental health hazards). Because the processes of poverty and racial segregation are intertwined with neighborhood influences in shaping the context of child development they will be briefly discussed in terms of their associations with child and family outcome.

Poor neighborhoods are disproportionately part of the life experiences of children who are already facing other important threats to their development. In the Northeast and the North central regions of the USA, the concentration of poor families in the inner city has risen (Jargowsky & Bane, 1990; Wilson, 1991, 1994). In 1991, 24.0 % of all children age six years and under were poor and the corresponding figure for African American children was 51.2% (U.S. Bureau of the Census, 1992). Because, children of African American families are over represented among the poor, they have a higher probability of residing in inner city neighborhoods (Wilson,

1991) and of experiencing chronic poverty, both conditions presenting high risks to their development (Chase- Lansdale, Brooks-Gunn, & Zamsky, 1994; Duncan, Brooks-Gunn, & Klebanov, 1994; Huston, 1991).

Very poor neighborhoods are usually populated by women and small children. A large number of the women are single and on welfare (Anderson, 1991). Studies have found that children raised in single-parent households are more likely to present adjustment problems (Thomson, Hanson, & McLanahan, 1994) and, on average, do worse than other children in terms of educational attainment and family formation (Dornbusch et al., 1985; Garfinkel & McLanahan, 1986). Examining the geographical distribution of poverty in Cleveland, Coulton and Pandey (1992) found that the percentage of female-headed households, the percentage of substandard housing, and the crime rates in the neighborhood were the strongest predictors of risk for children's health and behavior. However, the mechanism by which these social conditions lead to poor outcomes for children is not clear. The issue is further complicated by the fact that single-mothers and their young children are the families most likely to experience long-term welfare dependence, and those whose children are at greatest risk for a lifetime of impoverishment (Bane & Ellwood, 1986; McLanahan & Booth, 1991).

In summary, it is difficult to disentangle the effects of neighborhood characteristics on family and child development from the processes of poverty, racial segregation, and the economic and social problems associated with living in single- parent families that simultaneously take place in these contexts.

Poverty and Child Development

Poverty has detrimental effects on children and families and often coexists with low levels of other parental resources (Brooks-Gunn, Klebanov, Liaw, & Duncan, 1995). A sizable body of research documents the deleterious consequences of growing up poor, such as impaired cognitive development, problems in socioemotional adjustment, and poor physical health (Brooks-Gunn & Furstenberg, 1986, 1987; Huston, Garcia-Coll, & McLoyd, 1994; McLeod & Shanahan, 1993; Sameroff & Seifer, 1995; West & Brick, 1991). Delays in cognitive development in the preschool years increase the likelihood of lower achievement in school, higher grade retention, and school dropout (Brooks-Gunn, Guo, & Furstenberg, 1993; Campbell & Ramey, 1994; Patterson, Kupersmidt, & Vaden, 1990). Similarly, early behavior problems are associated with subsequent emotional problems, such as poor peer relations, conduct disorders, depression and delinquency (Dodge, Pettit & Bates, 1994; Sampson & Laub, 1994).

Other studies report that children who are poor, or who have a history of poverty, have more mental health problems than non-poor children (McLeod & Shanahan, 1993). Their findings indicate that poverty is associated with depression and antisocial behavior in children. Children with histories of persistent poverty have higher rates of antisocial behaviors, which might be the result of exposure to unsafe or unhealthy environments.

The health, well-being, and developmental status of children from families that receive public assistance income (i.e., Aid for Families with Dependent Children, AFDC) are less auspicious, on average, than those of children from families that are neither poor nor on welfare (Zill, Moore, Smith, Stief, & Coiro, 1995). Children in long-term welfare families have more developmental problems than those dependent for a short period. Findings from Zill et al. also indicate that the home environments of the former group tend to be less conducive to child health and safety. Although the influences of the home environment of children living in poverty and the interactions with their parents have been studied in terms of their contribution to developmental outcome, the contribution of the neighborhood context in which these families reside has not received much attention.

Another line of evidence indicates that poverty increases the risk of violence toward children (Gelles, 1992; Pelton,

1994). For example, criminal victimization is more common among poor children (Schubiner, Scott, & Tzelepis, 1993). Findings from two national surveys on family violence indicate that the rate of severe violence was 62.0 % and 46.0 % higher in poverty-level than in non-poverty families (Gelles, 1992). Further, poverty has a stronger association with women's risk of using abusive violence toward their children than it has for men. This is likely due to the fact that the prevailing cultural norm is still for women to be responsible for much, if not all, of child care and child rearing. Poverty is also more strongly related to abusive violence in specific circumstances—young children, younger caretakers, and single parent status.

Poverty is associated with dangerous conditions in and around the home (Zill et al., 1995). Impoverished families frequently live in neighborhoods with the highest crime rates, in apartments that are not secure, and in houses made dangerous by health and safety hazards such as lack of heating, poor wiring, and exposed lead paint. For example, Mierly and Baker (1983) found that the rate of residential fires, as well as the fatality rate from such fires is far greater in low-income areas than it is in middle-class neighborhoods. Cases of childhood lead poisoning have been concentrated in poor neighborhoods, and children's falls from windows have been concentrated among AFDC families (Pelton, 1989). Because poverty is increasingly intertwined with a number of negative neighborhood conditions (Chow & Coulton, 1992; Coulton & Pandey, 1992; Wilson, 1987), it is likely that its contribution to child development operates both through restricted resources available to individual families as well as through the macrostructural forces that shape poor communities. Fewer economic opportunities and resources in the neighborhood may limit parents' job prospects, reduce the number of marriageable men in the area (Wilson, 1991), and reduce the number and quality of services available for young children (e.g., types and quality of child care arrangements, availability of health care providers).

Poverty and Parental Behavior

Previous research has documented that economic hardship predicts how parents interact with their children. Parents who face persistent poverty usually experience greater stress and have fewer resources available to draw upon, both conditions increasing the likelihood of parental discord and harsh disciplinary practices. Socioeconomic disadvantage has an adverse effect on parenting behavior such that parental disorders and difficulties are more likely to develop, diminishing the capacity for supportive, consistent, and involved parenting (McLoyd, 1990). The use of punitive, coercive parenting styles may be associated with developmental outcome by increasing children's risk of antisocial behavior (Mrazek & Haggerty, 1994).

Examining the effects of economic difficulty on parents and children, Elder and Caspi (1988) found that in times of stressful economic conditions aversive interactions between parents and children increased, whereas the ability of parents to manage their children diminished. Lempers, Clark-Lempers, and Simmons (1989) also found that the indirect statistical effects of economic hardship worked through stress-induced changes in parental nurturance and discipline. In a more recent study of adolescent adjustment, Conger, Conger, Elder, Lorenz, Simons, and Whitbeck (1992) confirmed that economic hardship was linked to adolescent development largely through its association with parenting behavior. Objective economic conditions, including unstable work, were related to parents' emotional state and behavior through their perceptions of increased economic pressure and limited resources to cope with pressure. Economic stress was associated with demoralization in parents, which in turn was related to marital conflict and "bad" parenting—harsh, inconsistent discipline and hostile rejection or noninvolvement. It seems clear from the above discussion that as a family's economic situation worsens, parents exhibit less nurturance and more inconsistent discipline towards their children (Conger et al., 1992; Lempers et al., 1989; McLoyd & Wilson, 1991).

Other deleterious conditions of the neighborhood (e. g., threat of crime, lack of recreational facilities) may generate stressful experiences for the parents too and therefore, may be associated with direct and indirect threats to children's development. Fear among parents residing in high-crime areas may be similarly manifested in a restrictive and punitive style of discipline in an effort to protect children from the influences of negative forces in the neighborhood. Thus, parents' adaptations to dangerous environments may result in child-rearing strategies that impede normal development (Garbarino, Kostelny, & Dubrow, 1991) such as restricting exploratory play to avoid dangers. Restricted social activities reduce the opportunities that children have for social play, for socializing with peers, for attending day care, and for sharing quality time with family outside of the home (e.g., play activities). Further, in the presence of dangerous conditions, other threats to child development may rise from the fact that parents need to be more diligent in the supervision of their children, and have little leeway for lapses in responsibility, as compared to middle-class families.

In summary, within poverty contexts, financial hardship, physical and emotional problems of children and parents, health and safety hazards associated with deteriorated housing and neighborhoods, family tensions and social isolation are all factors that may increase the likelihood of adverse developmental outcomes for children. From the evidence reviewed above it follows that poverty and the conditions associated with it help predict the ways that parents interact with their children. It can be assumed that as parental stress increases the capacity for nurturing decreases, and the likelihood of adverse developmental consequences increases. Whether the stress stems from unemployment, insufficient income, a difficult child, inadequate housing, fear of crime, or the interaction of any of the former, these are circumstances in which parental competence can be diminished.

Parenting in the Context of Poor Inner-City Neighborhoods

How parents perceive, organize, and manage the world outside the household has not been studied extensively by sociologists or developmentalists interested in the socialization process. Traditional studies of family processes have been restricted to intra-familial interactions and exchanges. Developmentalists are accustomed to regarding child rearing as a dyadic, or at most, an interpersonal activity that takes place within families. Although not wrong, this perspective is incomplete because it ignores the fact that styles of parenting can be an adaptation to conditions outside the household, specifically the social organization of the surrounding community (Furstenberg, 1993; Gephart, 1989). Because the context in which parenting occurs may influence both the parents' style of management and their success in implementing their socialization goals, parenting style in relation to extra-familial context may be equally consequential for child behavior and development.

McLoyd and Wilson (1991) have suggested that the parenting behaviors of African- American mothers may be particularly vulnerable to exposure to the multiple stressors of poverty and single parenting in the context of low-SES neighborhoods. Low-income, single, African American mothers who lived in low-SES neighborhoods provided less supervision of their children's behavior than other parents, and less supervision has been strongly associated with aggression and delinquency among youth (Hogan & Kitagawa, 1985; Wilson, 1996). Lower levels of supervision in the context of a low-SES neighborhood, where negative role models and deviant peers are accessible, might provide the ingredients conducive to fostering aggressive behavior in children. It may be assumed that the lower levels of parental supervision reported for low income, single African American mothers, in general, would not be associated with their children exhibiting heightened levels of aggression if they lived in middle-SES neighborhoods because it is less likely that these children would be exposed to deviant role models or peer groups. Alternatively, middle-SES neighborhoods may exhibit greater social organization, in the form of sharing collective responsibility for children and providing more adult monitoring.

Parental effectiveness is a key ingredient in the successful adaptation of impoverished children (Furstenberg, 1993; Jarrett, 1995). In an attempt to illustrate the connections between neighborhood characteristics and family functioning, Furstenberg (1993) used a methodology of "focused field-work" to study twelve families from poor neighborhoods in Philadelphia. Half of these families lived in relatively organized blocks and half lived on blocks that were less socially organized. Within each neighborhood there was tremendous variation in parental competence, e.g., differences in parents' child-rearing skills. As Furstenberg explains, certain parents were more successful than others in commanding respect, obtaining cooperation, and transmitting and implementing their goals—variations that will probably relate to developmental outcome in children. Apparently, certain features of the neighborhood environment conditioned parents' managerial skills by enhancing or interfering with parents' ability to implement goals for their children.

Furstenberg (1993) also found that parents are likely to have more success when they reside in communities where the burden of raising children is seen as a collective responsibility and where strong institutions sustain the efforts of parents. This view is consistent with the hypothesis of collective socialization, in which neighborhood role models and monitoring are important ingredients in a child's socialization process (Jencks & Meyer, 1990) and will be empirically tested in the current study. Socially approved behavior is thought to be reproduced by the presence of role models and mechanisms of social control employed by adults, thereby discouraging alternative forms of behavior (Furstenberg & Hughes, 1994). Neighborhoods low in social organization may offer fewer opportunities for families and children to become part of networks of social exchange. Parents in neighborhoods exhibiting greater social organization may be more likely to use other community members as resources in parenting.

In brief, results suggest that conditions in the neighborhood area interact with family characteristics (e.g., parental competence). Where parents live appears to affect how parents manage their children—their means of shielding their children from dangers and exposing them to opportunities (Anderson, 1991; Jarrett, 1995). By extension, the interplay between neighborhood and parenting process is probably associated with their children's success in averting serious problems and finding pathways out of poverty.

From the literature previously reviewed, it can be assumed that a configuration of organizational features of neighborhood—the extensiveness of social networks, social trust and perceived normative consensus on parenting, the availability of resources—all directly affect the support parents receive, either by reinforcing or attenuating the link between family and surrounding formal and informal institutions. According to Furstenberg (1993), the connectedness of the family in its immediate context shapes the strategies of parenting and is an index of the degree of collective socialization that takes place in the neighborhood.

To summarize, Furstenberg's findings (1993) suggest that different patterns of family management exist depending on the amount of institutional resources, social trust, and social control in the neighborhood. Parents' management strategies—particularly, the degree of reliance on support from the larger community—reflect their location in the surrounding community and the receptivity of local institutions to parental initiative. The mediating role of parenting behavior in combination with exposure to particular opportunity structures in the neighborhood may explain children's developmental functioning. The neighborhood context may interact with different levels of parental competence to create different styles of family management, with, perhaps, varying developmental outcomes for children. The availability of resources, the degree of normative consensus, and the strength of social bonds forged by kinship and friendship, may all contribute to a close connection between local institutions and the family (Walker & Furstenberg, 1994).

Residential mobility

Furstenberg (1993) has described the social processes triggered by the strategies that families use to cope with worsening conditions of the neighborhood. A primary strategy of families in transitional communities is geographical mobility. Changes at the community level (i.e., lack of embeddedness in social networks, lack of perceived consensus) help to bring about the disengagement of the family from the community. The family becomes less and less embedded in formal and informal structures that reinforce parental standards with systems of formal and informal control becoming attenuated. A growing number of parents begin to display stringent parental monitoring practices (Brodsky, 1996; Jarrett, 1995) more characteristic of anomic areas, such as chaperonage and confinement. These parental strategies to cope with dangerous neighborhoods may be practically sensible but the side effects on children's development may be detrimental in the long run (Garbarino et al., 1991).

A second strategy seen in transitional neighborhoods is a shift from collective to individualistic strategies. Fewer parents are willing to delegate authority to formal institutions that have lost their credibility and command of external resources. Because of high residential mobility, and lack of embeddedness of the family in the community, informal networks become attenuated as close friends and kin move out and are replaced by new residents who are regarded as outsiders. The perception of normative consensus in the community diminishes accordingly. As parents come to believe that their standards for child rearing are not shared by others, they begin to distrust other families nearby. The social world of transitional communities may contract as neighbors become strangers (Furstenberg, 1993).

The dynamics described by Furstenberg (1993) in transitional neighborhoods can be understood using social disorganization theory (Sampson, 1992) and reflect the transformation of socially organized communities into so-called underclass areas (Wilson, 1991). Furstenberg's observations support Wilson's (1991) description of community disintegration whereby stable families flee distressed areas leaving behind a contingent of demoralized parents to contend with a growing number of problem-ridden families.

Though illuminating, the above results come from cross-sectional analyses. The direct and indirect effects of neighborhood on child development need further examination in longitudinal research. Elaborating on Furstenberg's findings, it can be assumed that certain features of the neighborhood environment (e.g. perception of crime, availability of resources) condition parents' managerial skills. These aspects of the neighborhood context can enhance or interfere with parents' ability to implement goals for their children.

Two hypotheses may be advanced from the above findings: (1) perceived neighborhood context interacts with different levels of parental competence to create different styles of family management, with, perhaps, varying outcomes for children; and (2) children growing-up in families that are embedded in networks of social exchange within their neighborhoods should do better developmentally than children in families isolated from networks and resources.

Although the former hypotheses can be asserted from a theoretical point of view, and are consistent with findings from several studies (Anderson, 1991; Furstenberg, 1993; Jarrett, 1995) to date they have not been tested empirically.

Community Social Organization as a Framework

The concept of social organization can be used as a framework for understanding the effects of neighborhoods on individual outcomes (Sampson, 1992). Social organization refers to the extent to which the residents of a neighborhood are able to maintain effective social control and realize their common values (Kasarda & Janowitz, 1974). Two major dimensions of neighborhood social organization are: (a) the prevalence, strength, and interdependence of social networks in a community—both informal (e.g., density of acquaintanceship; intergenerational ties) and formal (e.g., organizational participation), and (b) the extent of collective supervision that the residents direct and the personal responsibility they assume in addressing neighborhood problems. Both formal institutions and informal networks reflect social organization (Sampson, 1993).

Community social organization is strong to the degree that local structures are able to accomplish the goals of residents and exert social control from within the community (Sampson, 1992). This includes the protection and provision of resources for residents, the socialization of youth, and other functions associated with community life (Warren, 1980). Previous studies indicate that neighborhood social organization can be affected by the macro-structural influences that have operated in many cities in the 1980s—increase in poverty concentration, family disruption, and turnover of residents (Bursick & Grasmick, 1993). Further, studies have demonstrated that social organization within a community is diminished by poor economic status, ethnic heterogeneity, family disruption, and residential mobility (Sampson, 1991; Sampson & Groves, 1989). Ethnic heterogeneity and rapid population turnover prevent urban communities from organizing collectively against groups migrating into neighborhoods, or from adequately controlling the antisocial behavior of area residents (Bursick, 1988; Shaw & McKay, 1972). Heterogeneity and turnover also undermine ties between neighbors, limiting their ability to agree on a common set of values or to solve common problems (Bursick, 1988).

Changes occurring in the neighborhood social organization can affect individual behavior. For example, the rapid loss of population and resulting devastation of institutional and service networks have been correlated with poor health outcomes for children (Wallace, 1990). Two recent studies have found that neighborhood economic hardship (O'Campo,

Xue, Wang, & O'Brien, 1997; Roberts, 1997) and housing costs (Roberts, 1997) are positively associated with low birth weight. Interestingly, findings by O'Campo et al. also indicated that neighborhood macro-level factors interacted with individual-level risk factors for low birthweight, such that social class, poor housing conditions, unemployment rates and high crime modified the relationship between individual risk factors and low birthweight.

Neighborhoods with high levels of unemployment are more likely to experience problems of social disorganization (Sampson, 1987). High rates of joblessness trigger other problems in the neighborhood —ranging from crime, gang violence, and drug trafficking to family break-ups and problems in the organization of family life (Gephart, 1989). These in turn may diminish the density of social ties and undermine the effectiveness of institutions, social networks, household economies, and family functioning. Thus, the problems of family organization and neighborhood social organization in poverty neighborhoods can be thought of as mutually reinforcing.

Two kinds of social isolation may be distinguished in inner-city neighborhoods: (a) families who deliberately isolate themselves from other families (Brodsky , 1996; Jarrett, 1995), and (b) families who lack contact with institutions, families, and individuals in the larger mainstream society, regardless of the level of interaction with neighbors. Studies of the poor have indicated a paucity of ties within the immediate vicinity and a reliance on kin-based networks that may isolate them from their immediate community (Furstenberg, 1993). The low density of networks within the neighborhood may reduce the effectiveness of community controls and institutions (Sampson, 1991). Furthermore, as ever wider sections of major cities become impoverished (Jargowski & Bane, 1991) specific neighborhoods may become geographically isolated from mainstream influences and institutions that serve the wider community.

In other words, neighborhood social organization depends on the extent of local friendship ties, the degree of social cohesion, the level of resident participation in formal and informal voluntary organizations, the density and stability of formal organizations, and the nature of informal controls. Neighborhoods that integrate residents by an extensive set of obligations, expectations, and social networks are in a better position to control and supervise the activities and behavior of children and to monitor developments (i.e., the breaking up of congregations of youth on street corners and the supervision of youth leisure time activities) (Sampson, 1992).

The connection and stability of social networks in neighborhoods high in social organization transcend the household because neighborhood adults have the potential to observe, report on, and discuss the behavior of children in different circumstances. These networks reinforce the discipline the child receives in the home, because other adults in the neighborhood assume responsibility for the supervision of youth who are not their own (Sampson, 1992). This point of view is concordant with one of four theories outlined in Jencks and Mayer's (1990) taxonomy of neighborhood influences on child development, namely the collective socialization hypothesis, in which neighborhood role models and monitoring are considered an important ingredient to a child's socialization. That is, community adults—not just a child's parents—play an important role in promoting adaptive behaviors in children. The hypothesis assumes that the existence of informal networks of association in the neighborhood ensures that children are monitored by adults other than their parents, facilitating collective socialization. According to social organization theory, family embeddedness in social exchange networks within the neighborhood should be associated with positive behavioral outcomes in children.

Dense social networks within the community may also connect children with opportunities for modeling, mentoring, and sponsorship. The density of child contacts with adults who can offer social guidance and support is an important aspect of the child's position in the opportunity structure, especially if these adults can inform children of opportunities outside the neighborhood (Furstenberg & Hughes, 1994). Networks of reciprocal obligation and exchange are particularly important to child development when they exhibit intergenerational closure (i.e., which occurs when parents of children who are friends are themselves friends).

Particular aspects of community social organization, such as the ability of residents to guide the behaviors of others toward prosocial norms, density of local friendship networks, and the high levels of local participation in organizations have all been found to work against deviance (Sampson & Groves, 1989). Coleman (1988) uses the term "social capital" to refer to the community resources (i.e., norms, mutual obligations, and opportunities for sharing information) that support child development. According to this view, the neighborhood can be seen as a reservoir of social capital because its social relationships can serve as resources for parents to draw upon in implementing their goals.

Although specific aspects of community organization have not been examined directly in research on child development, studies on child maltreatment (Garbarino & Sherman, 1980) have shown that when people evaluated their neighborhoods as bad places to raise children, the rates of child maltreatment were the highest. Similarly, Furstenberg's (1993) ethnographies of neighborhoods with public housing indicate that parenting success was compromised by the fact that mothers seldom knew their neighbors, felt they did not share common values with them, and found few neighborhood organizations in which to participate.

From the previous discussion, it can be assumed that the qualities of the social environment are the proximal determinants of children's development. Thus, elaborating on the ideas advanced by Furstenberg and Hughes (1997) and by Sampson (1991; 1992) it is hypothesized that neighborhood infrastructure, demographic characteristics, and institutions will predict child development via its associations with family social relationships within the neighborhood. In Coleman's terms, to the extent that parents and children possess social capital in the neighborhood (i.e., embeddedness in social networks), the neighborhood may have more or less positive influence on their lives.

The purpose of the current study is twofold: (a) examine the longitudinal relationships among neighborhood structure (i.e., objective ratings of the neighborhood area), maternal perceptions of neighborhood characteristics, parenting, and the development of African American preschool children; and (b) report on the development and psychometric properties of a self-report scale designed to measure perceived affective, cognitive, and social dimensions of neighborhood life that are suitable for parents of young children.

Implications for Intervention

From an applied perspective, questions regarding whether and by what means the characteristics of the neighborhoods influence child development are not only of theoretical interest, but are also important to those formulating public policies addressing social inequality (Lynn & McGeary, 1990). Consistent with the ecological model, both researchers and practitioners have realized that neighborhoods are an important link between the family and society (Bursik & Grasmick, 1993; Warren, 1980), and they have written about the importance of targeting human service interventions to the neighborhood level (Barry, 1994; Cochran, Lerner, Riley, Gunnarsson, & Henderson, 1990).

The population of interest for the current study could be considered at-risk given environmental characteristics (poor, segregated, African American single parent, female-headed families) and as such, should receive top priority for preventive and/or ameliorative interventions. African American children are at greater risk for developmental problems (Dodge, Pettit, & Bates, 1994) probably related to various contextual factors such as inequities of racial discrimination and prejudice (Spencer, 1990), higher probability of being persistently poor (Duncan et al., 1994; McLoyd, 1990), and living in high-risk neighborhoods (Duncan et al., 1994; Kupersmidt et al.,1995).

The site of this study, Baltimore, had a large increase in neighborhood poverty from 1970 to 1980 (Jargowsky & Bane, 1990), and is one of the ten largest metropolitan areas in which African American families are very highly segregated (Massey & Denton, 1989; Massey & Hajnal, 1995) on several dimensions including evenness, exposure, clustering, centralization, and concentration. Such segregation isolates a minority group from amenities, opportunities, and resources that affect social and economic well-being (Massey & Denton, 1989), and may result in a more restricted social environment and less optimal development. Following Wilson's (1991) description we would expect Baltimore inner-city neighborhoods to be low on dimensions of social organization. However, this question needs to be addressed empirically. Depending on the sources of neighborhood data, it is important to determine whether residents' perceptions coincide with more objective descriptions of the neighborhood area in order to understand how neighborhood characteristics are related to family and child development.

DEVELOPMENT OF THE PERCEIVED NEIGHBORHOOD SCALE

Perspectives on the Measurement of Neighborhood Characteristics

The study of neighborhood ecology can be approached from two different perspectives: (a) subjective, encompassing the neighborhood as it is perceived by its residents, and (b) objective, as it is rated by external sources. As Burton, Price-Spratlen, and Spencer (1997) note, each approach has its strengths and its limitations.

Because quality of neighborhood depends on both its material and social resources, the present study will encompass both perspectives to understand the influences that neighborhood context has on the quality of parenting and developmental outcome of preschool children. The former is based on the observation that the very definition of the term neighborhood is often grounded in the subjective: a neighborhood is that through which an individual experiences society (Morris & Hess, 1975). For example, Furstenberg (1993) found that family members had considerable difficulty agreeing upon the precise geographical boundaries of the neighborhood (e.g., little consensus was found when drawing a neighborhood map both within and between families). Perceptions of neighborhood capture residents' personal evaluations of their social milieu.

Further, the concept of neighborhood seems to change according to use (i.e., for some purposes the neighborhood is the block, for others it encompasses a wider physical area including shopping, schools, and community facilities). Moreover, insofar as neighborhood has a geographical referent, its meaning depends upon context and function.

There is obviously an objective side to neighborhood, too—the availability of city services, the upkeep of houses and alleys, the congestion or openness of the area, the style of housing, and the way these influence neighborly exchanges. Neighborhood, as measured by geographical address, reflects physical and demographic properties.

The different facets of neighborhood have given rise to different strategies of assessment: (a) place, that views neighborhood as a site and attempts to understand the state of the area. For example, Bryant's (1985) definition limits the geographic border of neighborhood in terms of the walking distance of a young child; (b) network, that understands neighborhood in terms of interacting dimensions (i.e., neighborhood as a system of social networks); and (c) local culture, understands the traits of the area in terms of its folkways and behavioral norms (i.e., neighborhood as a subculture with shared social practices and beliefs).

These assessment strategies may have different utilities depending on the neighborhood phenomenon of interest (Burton, Price-Spratlen, & Spencer, 1997). The current study will build on the place approach to examine structural factors of the neighborhood geographic area, and on the network approach to study how sense of community, and embeddedness in networks of social exchange with neighbors are related to child development.

Measures of Neighborhood Context

Tienda (1991) contends that one of the main problems of research addressing the effects of neighborhoods on individuals is that researchers have not included the dimension of social interaction in their definition and measurement of neighborhood. Such interaction is often the implied mechanism through which neighborhoods are thought to affect individuals. Thus, poor people do not necessarily interact with their affluent neighbors simply because they live in the same census tract.

Most ethnographic accounts suggest considerable diversity within neighborhoods, with the implication that individuals may embed themselves in varying social networks within a neighborhood with dramatically different consequences. For example, Anderson (1989) and Jarrett (1995) report findings illustrating differences in outcome between adolescents who are "on the street" and those whose behavior is monitored and supervised by parents and other adults. Therefore, conclusions about neighborhood influences cannot rely solely on compositional statistics to understand the ways in which individual status and behavior are affected, but must also be based on residents' perceptions of the neighborhood environment.

Measures of neighborhood characteristics available in studies of inner-city families that use census tract data only may be relatively remote from individual perception and action, and therefore may be unlikely to reveal strong linkages between macrolevel neighborhood characteristics and outcomes for inner-city poor families. While it can be assumed that there is a direct way in which material conditions of living in poor neighborhoods are associated with adverse developmental consequences the relationship may be indirect, mediated by psychological processes. The current study will include an assessment of the individual perceptions and experiences of people in their neighborhoods, which being more variable, may help to explain why individuals living in the same neighborhood area may differ in regard to the developmental outcome of their children.

In order to capture how neighborhood characteristics are perceived and interpreted by parents the current study will assess more proximal characteristics of the neighborhoods, at the level of its social networks and organization as reflected in the residents' perceptions. It is expected that stronger linkages between neighborhoods and individual outcomes will emerge from characterizations of the perceived neighborhood—its opportunities, barriers, dangers, pressures and supports—as seen by its residents, rather than from distal factors.

The social dimension of neighborhood life (i.e., neighborhood networks, attachment, availability of resources) is included through the development of a measure of perceived neighborhood that assesses features of neighborhood life that have been recognized as important in the rearing of small children. Special consideration was given to including neighborhood dimensions that are pertinent to parenting, such as a parent's experience of isolation or involvement with others in the neighborhood (e.g., the frequency of neighbor-to-neighbor exchanges in the form of help giving and friendly social interactions such as greeting and visiting), social exchanges with neighbors who are also parents, participation in neighborhood organizations, availability of resources such as playgrounds and playmates for children, and threat of crime. According to the collective socialization hypothesis, both the strength and salience of bonds, and the sense of reciprocal obligations are family and community based resources that foster child development.

In summary, to examine the associations between family and neighborhood influences, the PNS assesses the dimension of social embeddedness of family members in the neighborhood. Other dimensions tapped by the scale are sense of community, satisfaction with neighborhood and perceived crime. Available evidence on the relationship between these dimensions and individual behavior will be discussed in the following sections.

Neighborhoods as Social Structures

A key issue for research on neighborhoods is the geographic and/or social unit that is used to define and circumscribe them. Are neighborhoods defined mainly or solely by geographical boundaries? A neighborhood is place and people (Morris & Hess, 1975). The concept of neighborhood includes spatial units, associational networks, and perceived environments (Gephart, 1997). Neighborhoods are physically bounded areas characterized by some degree of homogeneity and cohesion (Advisory Board on Child Abuse and Neglect, 1991; White, 1987). Coupled with the spatial dimension a neighborhood has a history (i.e., the evolution of residential patterns) and a psyche (i.e., some sense of shared identity among residents, as in a common inclination to name the neighborhood).

Bursick and Grasmick (1993) distinguish three features in a neighborhood. First, it is a physical (i.e., geographic area) and a social subset of a larger unit. Second, it has a collective life that emerges from the social networks that have arisen among the residents and the sets of institutional arrangements that overlap these networks (i.e., the neighborhood is inhabited by people who perceive themselves to have a common interest in the area, and to whom a common life is available). Third, the neighborhood has some tradition of identity and continuity over time. Efforts to respect the history component have led to three elements in the definition of neighborhoods: a social component (i.e., interaction patterns), a cognitive component (i.e., a common understanding of boundaries and identities), and an affective component (i.e., a set of shared feelings of belonging) (Unger & Wandersman, 1985). In brief, neighborhood life encompasses a complex array of phenomena of different order (i.e., cognitive, affective, social, and cultural) operating at different levels of analyses.

Neighborhood Functions

As a social structure a neighborhood may perform a diversity of functions for its residents. It may serve as:

1. An arena for informal interaction among residents, in which case it is said that the neighborhood is high in "neighborhood sociability". Sociability between neighbors serves to mitigate some of the depersonalizing influences of the urban environment and often provides a sense of social belonging for individuals.

2. A center for interpersonal influence, both overt and subtle. The focus of influence may range from the way one landscapes a yard to methods of child rearing and voting preferences. Through the process of continuous observation of neighbors, learning by imitation occurs.

3. A source of mutual aid. Exchange of help (i.e., exchanging goods and services of various kinds) among those living in close proximity in urban areas is another frequent and important function of neighborhood.

4. An organizational base. People living in a given locale may be joiners of many groups. A critical question to be asked of any neighborhood is whether it has local organizations that are for the neighborhood and are used by residents (e.g., block clubs). If a neighborhood has these groups, it functions as a political and organizational base.

5. A reference group. The neighborhood can be a basis of identity. Individuals may be guided and changed in their behavior and values as a result of what they understand to be the social norms of their neighbors. Mann (1970) argues that a neighborhood resident has expectations of a similar outlook on life amongst its neighbors, particularly insofar as life in the neighborhood itself is concerned.

6. A status arena, in the sense that a neighborhood may act as a mirror for personal achievement and well-being.

Neighborhoods differ in the extent to which they perform these functions and in their organization as well. Some are highly formalized and hierarchically structured units, in which people have fixed roles. Most neighborhoods however, are less structured. Although neighborhoods differ in many ways, a healthy neighborhood has pride in the neighborhood, care of homes, security for children, and mutual respect of residents.

With advances in technology, communication, and transportation a shift in the function of neighborhoods has been observed. In our highly mobile society many functions once performed in geographical neighborhoods are now accomplished through diverse and extended networks that include contacts at work, and at civic, religious, social and other organizations that extend far beyond our geographic area of residence. However, while people may belong to a variety of communities depending on their interests, people still belong to only one neighborhood based on where they live.

On the other hand, although many adults have trans-neighborhood affiliations that can limit their involvement in local communities, adult friendships still have a marked spatial concentration in many cities. For example, between 31 and 45% of the residents of Detroit indicated that a majority of their friends live within the same neighborhood (Huckfeldt, 1983). In the current sample 25.3 % of the participants reported having one close friend in the neighborhood, 42.5 % reported having two, and 32.2 % reported having 3 or more close friends.

There are several reasons to expect the residential neighborhood to continue to focus people's social interaction (Logan & Spitze, 1994). Spatial proximity makes it convenient to spend time with others in the neighborhood and creates common interests. Neighbors have the same access to jobs and shopping, they have the same exposure to threats of crime and receive the same protection from the police, and their children typically attend the same school. Neighborhoods are often socially homogeneous. Thus, neighbors typically share bonds of class, race and ethnicity, religion, and even kinship. The resulting mixture of instrumental connections, social homogeneity, and sentiment can be a powerful basis for collective action. From a cultural perspective, neighborhood influences may be more real than its members may recognize for the reason that a neighborhood has its own established social values, roles and patterns of acting. In this sense, a neighborhood constitutes what social scientists describe as a social system or social structure.

In Warren's view (1980), three elements constitute the social-structural characteristics of neighborhoods: (a) identity: how much people feel that they belong to a neighborhood and share common destiny with others, (b) interaction, how often and with what number of neighbors do people interact on the average during the year, and (c) linkages: number and type of linkages to the larger community (e.g., people having membership in outside groups).

For many middle- and upper-class families, the idea of a close-knit neighborhood as the basis for socialization has been relegated to nostalgia. However, lower-SES families have less opportunity to move about beyond their neighborhood and fewer connections beyond their immediate environment. Consequently, they are much more vulnerable to conditions within the limited geographic area in which they live (Chavis & Wandersman, 1990). By the same token, the quality of neighborhood may have much more impact on children than on adults, because neighborhood institutions and activities are a meaningful part of the child's social world and children cannot so readily escape their influences.

For the reasons discussed above, enhancing our knowledge regarding the importance of neighborhoods for low-income and minority families becomes critically important. It also has practical implications for designing interventions aimed at improving and maintaining the neighborhood.

To provide a theoretical framework for the development of the Perceived Neighborhood Scale, a review of existing knowledge of neighborhood dimensions and dynamics, and their relation to the behavior of residents will follow. By emphasizing the kind of social exchanges and the degree of collective organization that takes place among neighbors, the review will discuss neighborhood dimensions relevant to parents of small children.

Social Dimensions of Neighborhood

A neighborhood's character is determined by a host of factors, but most significantly, by the kinds of relations that neighbors have with each other (Kromkowski, 1976). The social component of neighborhoods includes both informal social supports (e.g., emotional, instrumental, and informational) and social networks (i.e., links to other people) and is central in terms of offering support and providing resources for coping with stressors at both the individual and the neighborhood level. For example, Cochran and Brassard (1979) found that the relationship parents have with other adults played a major role in helping them in their task of raising their children successfully. Cochran (1988) later found that expansion of the personal network of single mothers was positively associated with their children's performance in school.

Neighboring as a source of social support

Neighboring can be defined as the total amount of various forms of social interactions neighbors engage in (Unger & Wandersman, 1985). These interactions include informal talks and visits, borrowing and lending, helping each other in emergencies, and constitute sources of informational, instrumental, and emotional support. The potential of neighbors to serve as sources of mutual aid is related to length of residence, presence of children, and similarity among residents. Unger and Wandersman (1985) argue that research on the concept of neighboring should not be limited to the concept of social interaction, but broadened to include cognitive components (e.g., cognitive mapping and symbolic interaction), and affective components (e.g., sense of community and attachment to place).

Studies of neighboring done to date have mainly investigated the relationship between frequency of interaction and amount of social support residents provide to each other to cope with specific problems, to ameliorate neighborhood conditions, as well as in relation to neighborhood satisfaction (Weenig, Schmidt, & Midden, 1990). In other words, most of the research on neighboring has been concerned with the quantity of social interaction, often with the implicit assumption of a positive relationship between quantity of interaction and neighborhood cohesion and/or potential for social influence.

Neighborhoods are foci of emotional, social, and financial investments, and potential sources of friends for children and adults. There is a debate over whether neighboring of any form is still prominent in social networks. While acknowledging the largely unbounded nature of contemporary community, relations with neighbors are vital components of personal networks (Campbell & Lee, 1992) and comprise a potential source of social support (Gambrill & Paquin, 1992).

Apparently, people identify more with neighborhoods characterized by frequent neighboring activities and a relatively strong sense of community suggesting the interdependence of these neighborhood phenomena. Findings from a study in 8 lower- SES neighborhoods in the Netherlands (Weenig, Schmidt, & Midden, 1990) indicated that identification with the neighborhood was strongly related to neighborhood cohesion.

In summary, the neighborhood provides a setting in which people can belong and interact positively with each other. Belonging and interacting are important not only in their own right but also because they facilitate the development and expansion of informal networks among neighborhood residents. These networks appear important for the ability of parents to parent. Findings from two studies (Hashima & Amato,

1994; Jennings, Stagg, & Connors; 1991) suggest that parents' social support systems may influence their ability to handle stress and their parenting practices, which in turn, may affect children's well-being.

According to the collective socialization hypothesis, social exchanges with neighbors and embeddedness in neighborhood networks constitute resources for ameliorating the stresses of poverty and /or enhancing the well-being of children and their families. Therefore, studies of neighborhood influence should measure the availability of social support, the extent to which there are informal networks in the community (and the density and closure of these networks), and the opportunities for information that exist in social relationships within the neighborhood.

Neighbors as social support providers

Neighbors typically exchange services (e.g., baby sitting, grocery shopping, information giving, borrowing of tools and food, crime prevention) of an inexpensive, emergency nature and serve as safety nets when other resources fail. For example, neighbors turn to each other for help before seeking contact with formal helpers (Warren, 1980). Neighbors have 3 advantages over other kinds of relationships: (1) due to face-to-face contact, a neighbor can respond speedily; (2) neighbors share common governmental resources and can band together when problems occur; (3) face-to-face contact offers opportunities for learning that may not be available from extended kin or friends (Litwak & Szeleny, 1969).

Other studies have reported that neighbors played a significant role in assistance with child care problems among single parents living in a black lower-class neighborhood (Korte, 1983), and among single mothers on AFDC (Belle, 1982; Sarri, 1988). Stack (1974) reported considerable helping behaviors exchanged among poor black families. Similarly, Campbell and Lee (1992) found that lower SES African Americans have neighborhood ties of longer standing and greater intimacy, which are characterized by more frequent contact than those of lower-SES whites. These results lend support to the social integration/need perspective. That is, for low-SES persons, longer-standing friendships and greater frequency of interaction with their neighbors appear to compensate for the looser weave of their lives into the collective beyond their neighborhood.

Neighbors are necessary supports to many single parent families with resource deficits, and to many two-parent families in which both parents work. The child maltreatment literature reports that parents who abuse or neglect their children are often lonely and isolated (Garbarino & Gilliam, 1980; Gaudin, Polansky, Kilpatrick, & Shilton, 1993; Polansky, Gaudin, Ammons, & Davis, 1988). They have smaller social networks and less supportive links with neighbors and friends than do other parents (Gaudin & Pollane, 1983; Salzinger, Kaflan & Artemyeff, 1983).

Neighbors can also provide emotional support in the form of socializing and companionship. By greeting and visiting each other, neighbors build a sense of social belonging and thereby increase their feeling of comfort in the neighborhood. Deep friendship and emotionally sustaining discussions between neighbors can strengthen attachment to and satisfaction with a neighborhood (Unger & Wandersman, 1985). Neighbors also share advice and guidance (informational support), therefore conveying a set of norms regarding home decoration, entertainment, child care and voting preferences (Unger & Wandersman, 1985). The latter is related to the degree of social control exerted by neighbors and depends on a number of factors such as agreement on values, shared interests and resources, a willingness to take action when violations of norms occur, and opportunities to monitor behavior (DuBow & Emmons, 1981). The potential for neighborhood social control has been signaled as an important protection against deviance and crime (Sampson, 1992).

Neighbors can play a role by directly providing resources, and by relieving daily hassles and crises that are related to the quality of family interaction. For example, Jennings, Stagg, and Connors (1991) found that mothers who are satisfied with their social support, praise their children more often and are less controlling than dissatisfied mothers. These findings suggest that parental competence may vary in direct relation to the availability, satisfaction/quality, and use made of a family's supportive resources in the neighborhood area. Indeed, it has been found that mother's social support moderates the effects of daily hassles of parenting (Crnic & Greenberg, 1990).

Social support from neighbors may reduce the stress experienced by parents living in poverty. Studying the associations between poverty, social support, and parental behavior, Hashima and Amato (1994) assessed three dimensions of social support (i.e., perceived availability, frequency of social interaction, and level of assistance actually received from others) and found that for low-income families, perceived social support buffered the effects of stressful conditions of poverty, and decreased the incidence of problematic parental behavior. Regardless of income level, help received from others (particularly in the form of assistance with children) decreased the incidence of unsupportive parental behavior thus demonstrating a main effect of social support.

In summary, parents' social support systems may influence their ability to handle stress and their parenting practices, which in turn may be associated with children's well-being. Because of its buffering properties (Cohen & Wills, 1985; Seagull, 1985), social support may alleviate the stressful effects that living in poor and dangerous neighborhoods have on the incidence of negative parental behavior, and therefore, protect child development. However, further research is needed to better understand possible associations between neighborhood support, parenting processes, and child development within the contexts of poor neighborhoods. This knowledge will provide informed suggestions to family-based interventions.

Affective Dimensions of Neighborhood

The affective dimension includes a sense of mutual help, a sense of community and attachment to place (Ringel &

Finkelstein, 1992). The sense of mutual help involves the belief that assistance is available when needed, even when neighbors are not frequently contacted. Thus, neighborhood perceived support can be understood in terms of confidence rather than utilization. Attachment to place develops through an analysis by individuals in their neighborhood in which the costs and benefits of living in their neighborhood are compared with other neighborhoods.

Sense of community

As defined by Sarason (1974), a sense of community encompasses feelings of membership and belongingness and shared socioemotional ties with others in the neighborhood. A decade later, Chavis, Hogge, McMillan, & Wandersman (1986) added an element of active commitment to the definition presented by Sarason. In their terms, psychological sense of community refers to a feeling that members have of belonging and being important to each other, and a shared faith that members' needs will be met by their commitment to be together (Chavis et al., 1986).

Mc Millan and Chavis (1986) include 4 elements in their definition of sense of community: membership (i.e., belonging to a group, boundaries that define "in" and "out" groups), mutual influence (i.e., the community influences the individual, and the individual influences the community), fulfillment of mutual needs (i.e., sense of cohesion when individual needs are met), and shared emotional connection (i.e., evolves through a shared history, positive experiences). These elements have been found related to length of residency, satisfaction with the community, and the number of neighbors one can identify by first name (Glynn, 1981).

Similarly, Riger and Lavrakas (1981) studied sense of community as reflected in neighborhood attachment and found 2 empirically distinct but correlated factors: social bonding (i.e., ability to identify neighbors and feeling part of the neighborhood) related to McMillan and Chavis's (1986) membership component, and behavioral rootedness (i.e., length of residence, home ownership), probably related to the shared emotional connection component described by McMillan & Chavis.

An important element present in both Sarason's (1974) and Mc Millan and Chavis's (1986) definitions of sense of community is the perception of similarity and acknowledged interdependence with others, a sentiment that has been signaled as an important ingredient in the socialization of children (Furstenberg, 1993) because of its potential to generate social trust, shared values, and normative consensus. Consistent with the former, in a study of resilient mothers living in risky neighborhoods Brodsky (1996) found that mothers' perceptions of differences in personal investments among neighbors did not generate feelings of close membership that are conducive to social trust. Instead, perceptions of lack of consensus and lack of shared values between mothers and their communities were associated with a negative sense of community.

Studies also suggest that children appear to facilitate local ties and involvement with neighbors (Gerson et al., 1977; Unger & Wandersman, 1982). That is, having children often requires that more time is spent in the neighborhood, and creates opportunities for receiving and providing help and advice. These social exchanges may constitute a source of self-definition and normative consensus. Gerson, Steuve, and Fisher (1977) found a positive association between family life cycle stage (i.e., families with small children) and sense of community, through increased social exchanges among neighbors. In brief, children appear to be an important consideration for associating or not associating with neighborhood activities and organizations.

However, Brodsky's (1996) findings highlight the potential benefits of limiting or creating barriers to neighborly exchanges when parents perceive the neighborhood as having a pervasive negative influence on their children. These findings illustrate what Jarrett (1995) described as the community bridging family pattern, a strategy characterized by restricted community relations and the enforcement of stringent parental monitoring found in poor families that promote social mobility in African American youth. To summarize, because of mixed findings regarding the potential benefits of social exchanges and sense of community in high-risk neighborhoods, the nature of the association between sense of community and child development needs to be further examined.

Attachment to neighborhood

People can feel more or less connected to the neighborhood in which they live. According to the systemic approach to urban organization (Berry & Kasarda, 1977), the length of time that a person has resided in an area is a key component of neighborhood attachment. Since it takes some period of time to develop extensive friendship, kinship and associational ties within a neighborhood, people would become increasingly embedded within the local networks of affiliation over time. In turn, these attachments would foster increased levels of identification with and positive sentiment directed toward the neighborhood. Kasarda and Janowitz (1974) presented results that supported the argument that length of residence is positively related to the number of friends, relatives and acquaintances who lived in the neighborhood, to participation in local organizations, and to sentiment toward the community.

Cochran, Lerner, Riley, Gunnarsson and Henderson (1990) argue that housing ownership is a critical factor in the stability of neighborhoods and the ability of parents to form individual support networks. Similarly, Campbell and Lee (1992) found that long-time neighborhood residents had larger networks of more intense relationships. When families are constantly moving, it is very hard to establish and maintain friendships and support networks. Renting tends to be associated with high residential mobility among the poor, and therefore, with lower commitment to the appearance of the buildings they live in.

As stated above, neighborhood influences assume some degree of social interaction among residents. However, the quantity and quality of social interaction within a neighborhood are the result of investments in social relationships by those living in the neighborhood (i.e., the degree to which parents invest in the neighborhood). Residential mobility may reduce the attachment to local community and the perceived incentive to invest in social relationships, and affect the way parents relate to their local environments, how they draw upon resources in their neighborhood, and how they manage and shape the child's milieu.

Studies need to address the issue of residential mobility, ideally by measuring exposure to the social environments that allegedly influence individual behavior. This is important in light of the evidence that chronically poor people change their residence frequently. For individuals who have changed residences, information about changes in the characteristics of their neighborhoods and neighbors should be included. Information about mobility will be controlled for in the current study by tracking whether families moved from age three to age five, and if they did, whether they moved to the same or to a different neighborhood. Changes in perceptions of neighborhood associated with household moves will also be explored.

Cognitive Dimensions of Neighborhood

The cognitive component of a neighborhood refers to the ideas and thoughts that individuals have about their neighborhood's social and physical environment. This cognitive component can be used both to understand the neighborhood and to develop ways of dealing effectively with neighborhood issues. One aspect of the neighborhood cognition involves a mental mapping process resulting from repeated experiences in the neighborhood, thus allowing individuals to better manage their neighborhood. For example, cognitive mapping in dangerous neighborhoods would determine where people felt safe to walk or where they could socially interact with others without fearing harm.

Perceived crime in the neighborhood

In the last decade it has become increasingly apparent that community violence is a more common feature of the environment in which children are growing up (Bell & Jenkins, 1993; Cicchetti & Lynch, 1993 ; Garbarino, Kostelny & Dubrow, 1991; Schubiner, Scott, & Tzelepis, 1993) particularly in large inner-cities in which poor, minority populations are over represented. Fear of crime is concerned with people's emotional responses and feelings of vulnerability in the face of dangerous conditions or the possibility of victimization (Ferraro, 1994). Crime and the perception of crime-related problems may interfere with person-environment transactions influencing how freely people move about the places where they live (Lisa, Sanchirico, & Reed, 1988; Taylor, 1995).

It can be assumed that residents of neighborhoods share a common goal of living in an area relatively free from the threat of crime (Bursik & Grasmick, 1993). A key function of the neighborhood is to provide a place of relative safety for its residents. Crime represents a very pervasive threat to neighborhood life. The increase in reported fear of crime over the recent decades (Clemente & Kleiman, 1977; Skogan, 1990; Taylor & Covington, 1993) suggests that for many people this basic protective function of the neighborhood is not met. Furthermore, some groups such as women, children, and the elderly who are more vulnerable to the effects of poor quality of the community environment may be more affected by the psychological consequences of fear of crime than others. Women, for example, report significantly more fear of crime than men (White, Kasl, Zahner, & Will, 1987). Fear of crime is also greater among African Americans, older people and persons living in urban areas (Gordon, Riger, Lebailly, & Heath, 1980).

Fear of crime is a serious individual- and community-level problem. At the family level, it can be assumed that elevated levels of crime virtually cut off basic human interaction of the type needed to develop and maintain the support networks required to successfully raise children. For parents living in dangerous neighborhoods, sheer survival for themselves and their children becomes an all-consuming preoccupation (Garbarino, Kostelny, & Dubrow, 1992). Brodsky (1996) found that lack of physical and emotional safety was an important barrier for membership and limited the chances for positive interactions among mothers living in risky neighborhoods. Moreover, neighborhood violence and crime are likely to affect the parenting styles of socialization, the decisions parents make regarding their children's social activities and their choice of friends. It can be assumed that neighborhood crime generates worries and concerns regarding personal and family safety; therefore, studies that assess the effects of frequent exposure or threat of exposure to violence on the quality of life of non-violent residents are needed.

However, the relationship between fear of crime and social interaction is far from clear. Little systematic study of the psychological consequences of crime has been done. Taylor, Gottfredson, and Brower (1985) found that actual and perceived measures of crime did not influence local social involvement. Similarly, a study by Lawton, Nahemov and Yeh (1980) found no relationship between rated fear of crime and indexes of well-being (activity participation, morale, friendship behavior), except housing satisfaction. However, the validity of the measures used in this study can be questioned.

Fear of crime is embedded in a broader set of perceptions of social disorder in the residential environment. Perceived crime is related to signs of disorder, which are crime-related factors and include manifestation of physical deterioration (e.g., vacant or dilapidated housing, trashy vacant lots, extensive litter and graffiti) as well as social events suggesting trouble (e.g., groups of people hanging out, public drug use or drug dealing, street hassles). In a study of 63 blocks in 12 neighborhoods in Baltimore, Taylor, Gottfredson, and Brower (1985) found that perceived minor crime problems inhibited feelings of emotional investment in the neighborhood. Research suggests that the physical deterioration of the neighborhoods may heighten the perception of the neighborhood as a dangerous place. In a study of 4 neighborhoods in Chicago, Lewis and Maxfield (1980) found that the presence of actual crime combined with what they called "symbols of uncivility" (e.g., abandoned buildings, physical deterioration, teenage loitering, drug use on the streets) increased the likelihood of residents reporting problems with crime in their neighborhood. These observations suggest an interactive relationship between fear of crime and the quality of the physical environment: poor-quality environments may trigger the perception that the neighborhood is a dangerous place while good-quality environments may attenuate the perception of danger. White, Kasl, Zahner, and Will (1987) speculate that this association exists because crime and poor physical conditions make parallel statements to residents about the social order of their neighborhoods. The perception of neighborhood crime can be seen as indication of a breakdown in social order (i.e., sense of the inability of a group to regulate itself).

Skogan (1990) states that people will make broad inferences about the presence of social and crime-related problems based on local physical incivilities. Physical incivilities include such environmental stimuli as graffiti, vandalism, vacant or dilapidated housing, abandoned cars, litter, and unkempt lots. As physical incivilities proliferate, residents perceive more problems in the locale and lose confidence in their neighborhood and in the police's ability to prevent or to control lawlessness, resident-based informal social controls weaken, residents become more fearful, criminals from adjoining areas are attracted to the locale, and the downward spiral becomes self-reinforcing (Skogan, 1990). Social incivilities include loitering youths, prostitutes or homeless people, rowdy behavior, drug dealing, and public drunkness. In support of Skogan's model, Perkins, Meeks, and Taylor (1992) found that physical incivilities are linked to the perception of social problems and crime.

Crime and social control

Social control is the ability of a social group or collectivity to engage in self-regulation (Janowitz, 1978). Therefore, social control represents the effort of the community to regulate itself and the behavior of residents. The capacity of local residents to regulate the nature of the activities that take place within the borders of their local communities is determined by the extensiveness and density of the formal and informal networks within the neighborhood that bind the residents together as a social community (Bursik & Grasmick, 1993). A central underlying dynamic of neighborhood social control is the attempt to protect the area from threats that may undermine its regulatory ability. Differential rates of criminal behavior and victimization among neighborhoods, and the resulting fear of crime that may develop among the residents of crime-ridden areas, represent variations in the ability of neighborhoods to regulate themselves through these networks. The success of such efforts is central to the perception of the quality of life within an area and provides a key context for the interpretation and evaluation of all other activities.

Ecological forces acting on a neighborhood such as expanding central business district, economic decline, or changes in racial settlement patterns play a significant role in weakening neighborhood controls. Neighborhood changes may result in elevated community concern and a wider incidence of physical decay and unsupervised teen groups which, in turn, lead to higher fear levels (Lewis & Maxfield, 1980; Skogan, 1986). Cross-sectional studies have provided support for the association between rapid community change and fear of crime (Covington & Taylor, 1991; Perkins, Meeks, & Taylor, 1992). However, findings from a longitudinal study (Taylor & Covington, 1993) suggest that the effects of rapid neighborhood change do not operate directly on fear. Instead, changes in a neighborhood's urban ecology shape its structural characteristics such as racial and age groups composition. The latter weave their own consequences which arise from urban property relations and other structural dynamics.

Shaw and McKay (1969) argued that 3 structural factors— low SES, ethnic heterogeneity, and residential mobility—led to the disruption of local community social organization, which in turn accounted for variations in crime and delinquency. If the ability of a neighborhood to regulate itself decreases, the likelihood that its residents will either engage in crime or become victims of crime will increase. The fact that sources of threat to neighborhood life are both internal as well as external (Rand, 1986) creates some special difficulties in understanding attempts to control crime. However, as Bursik (1986) and Skogan (1990) suggest, this is not a simple linear process. Higher crime rates can also disrupt the capacity for maintaining control in the neighborhood. For example, neighbors may withdraw from participation in community affairs because of their heightened fear and anxiety. If such withdrawal from local networks becomes widespread, the sense of mutual responsibility among the residents is undermined, and those who are able to do so may attempt to physically abandon the neighborhood at the earliest possibility (Skogan, 1990). As a result, the capacity for local control may further deteriorate, thereby accelerating the process that originally gave rise to crime.

To summarize, little is known about the direct and indirect effects of neighborhood perceptions of crime and how these may relate to child development. Therefore, it is critical that researchers in child development apply themselves to identify the effects that danger in the environment has on children's development, and to study the restraints that crime and drugs provide to inner-city residents in their parental competence. The current study will explore the influences that maternal perceptions of crime in the neighborhood have on children's development.

CHAPTER 3

Method

The study had two main purposes. First, to examine the psychometric properties of a measure of perceived neighborhood context at two points in time (i.e., age three and age five). Second, to test multilevel models of linear relationships among neighborhood, family, and child development variables. Specifically, longitudinal (i.e., age three to age five) and cross-sectional (i.e., age five) models were tested to examine the relationships between *structural characteristics of the neighborhood* (i.e., poverty rate, unemployment, percentage of female-headed households, residential mobility, and vacant housing) and *perceived characteristics of the neighborhood* (i.e., social embeddedness in neighborhood networks, sense of community, satisfaction with neighborhood, and perceived crime) as they relate to parenting and development of African American children. The variables studied are depicted in Table 1.

Table 1. Variables for the Longitudinal Model of Neighborhood Characteristics and Child Development.

Context	Predictors	Mediators	Outcome
Age 3 African American Low-SES families	*Age 3* Perceived neighborhood: social exchanges, sense of community, satisfaction, and perceived crime	*Age 4* Parenting style	*Age 5* Cognitive development Social development
Controlled for: Maternal education	Neighborhood structure: Census tract ratings of poverty, unemployment, female-headed families with young children, residential mobility, and vacant housing		

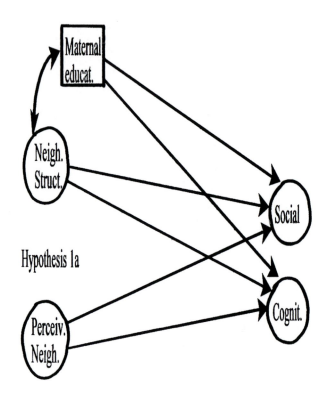

Hypothesis 1a

Hypothesis 1b

Figure 1. Models for Hypotheses 1a and 1b.

HYPOTHESES

An assumption of the current study is that the influence of neighborhood structure properties on developmental outcome operates indirectly through more proximal family- level determinants of development (i.e., perceptions of neighborhood context, family resources). Because family-level variables are thought to represent proximal influences on behavior, it was predicted that they would act as mediators of neighborhood influences. Therefore, the following hypotheses were tested:

Hypothesis 1a. Neighborhood structure (as measured by indexes of poverty, unemployment, female-headed households, mobility, and vacant housing) at age three is related to children's development at age five (see Fig. 1).

Hypothesis 1b. Perceived neighborhood (as measured by maternal responses to the Perceived Neighborhood Scale scores) at age three is related to children's development at age five (see Fig. 1).

Hypothesis 2. The statistical effects of neighborhood structure on children's development at age five are mediated by maternal perceptions of the neighborhood context (see Fig. 2).

Hypothesis 3. The statistical effects of maternal perceptions of neighborhood context at age three on development (i.e., social development) at age five are mediated by parenting style at age four (see Fig. 2).

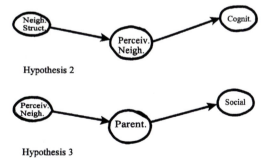

Figure 2. Models of Hypotheses 2 and 3

DATA AND SAMPLE

The data for this research consist of family-level and census-level data, and derive from four sources: (a) census ratings, (b) self-report (i.e., mothers' reports of family characteristics), (c) observers' ratings of parent-child interaction, and (d) standardized assessments of children's development.

The individual-level data were drawn from the database of an ongoing longitudinal investigation of child and family development. Data from families were collected at three points in time; that is, when children were three, four, and five years old. All data were collected prior to the passage of the Welfare Reform Act of 1996.

Study participants were recruited from three pediatric clinics serving low income, urban families. Eligibility criteria for the children included no history of major perinatal complications and the absence of congenital disorders or chronic illnesses. Approximately 26 % of the children were recruited from a growth and nutrition clinic and had a history of nonorganic failure to thrive; 29 % were recruited from a clinic that serves children at high risk for HIV infection, primarily through maternal drug abuse; and 44 % were recruited from a general pediatric primary care clinic. Families were matched for children's age, race, gender, and socioeconomic status.

Participants

The sample was a subset of a larger sample and included families with complete data at children's age three, age four, and age five. Participants were 129 African American families, the majority of whom were single-parent (92.2 %), female-headed households residing in low-income neighborhoods of Baltimore City. Most of these families received public assistance, including Medical Assistance (88.2%) and AFDC (83.5%). The majority of the mothers in the sample were neither married (74.4%) nor employed (76.4%). Participant mothers had a mean age of 27.64 years (SD = 5.70) at the onset of the study, and had completed a mean of 11.49 (SD = 1.41) years of education. Table 2 depicts demographic characteristics of the sample.

Analyses of demographic differences among groups within the sample indicated no significant differences for maternal education (df = 2, MS = .59, F =.30, p = .74; N = 129), employment (df = 2, χ^2 = 3.85, p < .15; N = 129), and parenting status (df = 2, χ^2 = .23, p < .74; N = 129). However, a significant difference in maternal age (df = 2, MS = 169.00, F = 5.57, p = .005; n = 129) was found indicating that mothers recruited from the growth and nutrition clinic were older.

Children in the sample were predominantly female (55 %) and had a mean age of 37.0 months (SD = 2.2).

Table 2. *Sample Characteristics* (*N* = 129)

	Mean	SD	Range
Characteristics of Mothers			
Age in years	27.6	5.7	15.9–41.6
Educatiion (in years)	11.5	1.4	7.0–16.0
Marital status: single	74.4a		
Public Assistance			
Medical assistance	88.2a		
AFDC	83.5a		
Single parents	92.2		
Characteristics of Children			
Age (in months)	37.0	2.2	34.0–45.0
Gender			
Males	45.0a		
Females	55.0a		
Race			
African American	100.0a		

a Expressed as percentage

Procedure

Mothers of children meeting eligibility criteria were invited to participate in a longitudinal clinical research project. Informed consent was obtained using procedures approved by the University of Maryland Institutional Review Board. The participation rate was 90%.

Laboratory visits were scheduled annually as close to the child's birthday as possible. For each annual visit, the laboratory evaluation included a developmental assessment, a video-taped observation of the mother and child, and a 60-90 min interview in which standardized questionnaires were administered including demographic information and parent and family functioning. The developmental assessment was administered by a trained psychologist or graduate student. The mother and child were videotaped for 10-min playing with blocks and reading a book, and mothers were requested to behave as they did at home. The camera was visible in the room but did not require an operator. Questionnaires were administered orally to control for varying literacy levels. Mothers were paid $25 for their participation, time, and transportation.

MEASURES

Structural characteristics of the neighborhood area were assessed by geocode variables construed by matching family addresses to a 1990 Census neighborhood identifier (files containing data at levels of tract). Thus, neighborhood structure variables were represented by census tract data. The census tract was used as the unit of analysis because it was the smallest geographic area for which data were available. Relevant addresses were taken at the time of child's fourth year visit.

Sample participants were distributed across 66 census tracts in Baltimore city. Descriptive analysis of the census variables indicated that the majority (72.1 %) of the families were concentrated in 39 tracts that correspond to the Baltimore city communities of West Baltimore, East Baltimore, Rosemont, Irvington, and Cherry Hill.

Approximately forty percent of the sample (n = 52) resided in West Baltimore, a large city area comprising 18 census tracts. Another ten percent of the sample (n = 14) resided in East Baltimore, an area comprising nine census tracts. According to the information available from the Baltimore City Planning Department, the population of these two communities can be characterized as low income (i.e., the percentage of households with public assistance income is 13.6 %) and predominantly African American (i.e., the percentage of African American population ranges from 83.8 % to 91.6 %). Within these communities, a percentage ranging from 16.3 % to 16.6 % of the population consists of children between 1- 9 years of age.

Two criteria were used to select census tract variables relevant to the development of preschool children. First, factors representing neighborhood characteristics identified in the literature as relevant for parenting and child development were selected (Duncan, Brooks-Gunn & Klebanov, 1994; Korbin & Coulton, 1997; McLoyd, 1998). Second, among the former, variables showing greater variability within the sample were chosen. As a result, the following census tract variables were used to represent neighborhood structure: percentage of persons below poverty, percentage of households with public assistance income, percentage of female-headed families with children, percentage of persons ≥ 16 years unemployed, male unemployment rate, percentage of people not living in the same household as 5 years ago (residential mobility), and percentage of rental housing units.

Under the rubric of demographics, controls for mother's education (measured as years of formal schooling) were included in all models fitted because of the association between this variable and child development.

Perceived Neighborhood Scale

A self-report scale that assesses maternal perceptions of neighborhood life that are relevant to parents of small children (i.e., embeddedness in social networks, sense of community, satisfaction with neighborhood and availability of resources, and perceived crime) was developed. The scale consists of 42 items, the majority of which are phrased in the form of declarative statements. Respondents express their level of agreement using a 5-point Likert-type scale. Item responses (i.e., scores range from 1 to 5) were recoded as needed so that higher scores represented an increasing degree of the dimension assessed. For the social embeddedness, sense of community, and satisfaction dimensions, higher values represent positive attributes, whereas for the perceived crime dimension low scores represent positive attributes. This scale was administered to mothers at two points in time, when their children were three (Time 3) and five (Time 5) years old.

The following steps were undertaken to develop the scale. First, available literature on neighborhood dimensions was extensively reviewed and four constructs were selected to be included in the scale because of their relevance to parenting: (a) social embeddedness in neighborhood networks—social activities that neighbors engage in, linkages that residents develop including both formal and informal exchanges, and frequency of social interaction among neighbors (i.e., neighboring, availability of social support) (Crittenden, 1985; Garbarino & Crouter, 1978; Levitt, Weber, & Clark, 1986; Polansky, Gaudin, Ammons, & Davies, 1985; Unger & Wandersman, 1982); (b) sense of community—feelings of membership and belongingness, trust and mutual influence, and shared socioemotional ties with others in the neighborhood (Chavis, Hogge, McMillan, & Wandersman, 1986; Unger & Wandersman, 1985); (c) satisfaction with neighborhood—a cognitive-affective dimension that examines parents' evaluations of the physical environment (e.g., parents' evaluations of the quality of neighborhood as a place to raise children) as meeting their childbearing needs and goals and their use of available local resources (Coulton, Korbin, & Su, 1996; Garbarino & Sherman, 1980; Polansky, Gaudin, Ammons, & Davies, 1985; Ringel & Finkelstein, 1991); and (d) perceived crime—threat and occurrences of crime and perceptions of social disorder in the residential environment (Coulton et al., 1996; Lewis & Maxfield, 1980; Perkins, Florin, Rich, Wandersman, & Chavis, 1990; Taylor et al., 1985).

Second, items were written to assess these four dimensions. These items were examined individually and as a group. Four experts in community aspects of child development independently judged the face validity of the items, provided feedback on the overall adequacy of the scale, and suggested new items. In addition, a panel of three independent judges evaluated the assignment of each item to one of the four intended scales and judged the adequacy and clarity of items through successive versions of the scale. Items that had 80% agreement or better across all three judges were kept. This procedure increased the probability that each item would correlate highest with the scale for which it was intended and that the scale would have internal consistency.

Third, items were piloted to determine their clarity and feasibility. Protocols of the scale were piloted and difficulties encountered by respondents were documented and subsequently revised by the panel of experts.

This procedure resulted in an initial scale of 42 items. Eleven items measure social embeddedness within the neighborhood, including informal exchanges with neighbors, friendships, presence of family relatives, and formal participation in neighborhood activities. Seven items measure sense of community, that is, feelings of trust, attachment, and belongingness to the neighborhood. Eleven items assess the respondent's overall satisfaction with neighborhood conditions and his/her appraisal of neighborhood resources. Finally, 13 items assess threat of crime and perceived signs of disorder in the neighborhood.

Prior to hypothesis testing, the factor structure, reliability, and validity of the scale were analyzed. Maternal responses to the Perceived Neighborhood Scale at Time 3 and Time 5 were factor analyzed to see how items clustered together and to examine the dimensionality of the scale. Because scale items were based on theory and were constructed a priori, confirmatory factor analysis (CFA) was performed at each point in time. Four underlying factors were expected to emerge from the scale and the goodness of fit of the resulting solution was tested.

Both the internal consistency of the scale factors and the test-retest stability from Time 3 to Time 5 were examined by comparing the factor structure of the scale at each point in time. In the absence of a move or major change in family or life events, the factor solution from age three to age five was expected to replicate. The construct validity of the scale was explored by computing the correlations between census ratings of the neighborhood area at age four and maternal perceptions of neighborhood at age five, controlling for mobility.

The distinctiveness of the perceived neighborhood factors was explored by examining the correlations between the scale factors and other psychological dimensions. For example, positive correlations were expected between perceived crime in the neighborhood and measures of maternal distress (i.e., maternal depression), between social embeddedness and measures of social support, and between sense of community and length of residence—operationalized as years living in the neighborhood.

Parenting style and social development

Measures for these constructs were coded from video-taped observations of mothers playing with their children. A coding system based on parenting style (Baumrind, 1971) was used to rate the continuous interaction of the mother and child over a 10-min observation period (Pratt, Kerig, Cowan, & Cowan, 1988). Individual items were coded using ordinal scores based on behaviorally defined anchors, with high scores representing the most positive interactions.

Videotapes of mother-child interaction were scored by two independent raters who were unaware of any characteristics of the families. Scoring was done through separate passes of the videotape by different raters. Different sets of raters rated the parent and the child variables. Raters were trained until agreement exceeded 90 % on 10 independently rated observations. Reliability was maintained at this level via weekly checks, with approximately 16% of the observations being double coded. Finn's r was calculated to determine levels of interrater reliability between raters for each factor on the scales. This statistic is free of problems such as chance agreement, additive bias, and homogeneity of between-subject variance. Agreement estimates using Finn's r exceeded .91 for all scales. Black, Dubowitz, and Starr (in press) reported internal consistency alpha coefficients above .80 for the maternal warmth and structure factors in a sample of the same longitudinal cohort.

Drawing on previous research on parental style and children's competence (Baumrind, 1996; Pratt et al., 1988), parenting style at age four was operationally defined as the degree of warmth/responsiveness and structure that mothers displayed in the videotaped interaction with their child. Following Cohn, Cowan, Cowan, and Pearson (1992), two scales were used to describe parenting style: maternal warmth/ responsiveness and maternal structure. Maternal warmth/responsiveness was assessed by three items tapping warmth (i.e., overall degree of warmth/coldness, overall pleasure/displeasure, and confidence in parental role) and two items tapping responsiveness (i.e., responsiveness and interactiveness). Maternal structure was assessed by four items (i.e., limit setting, structure, precision in use of language, and maturity demands of child). Both maternal warmth and structure ranged from minimal levels (low score) to optimal levels (high score). Scores on each item represent the typical level of the dimension displayed by the mother during the 10-min play interaction with the child.

Cohn et al. (1992) have reported adequate internal consistencies for their warmth/responsiveness and structure/control scales (i.e., α= .83 and α = .84 respectively). Internal consistencies for the current sample (N = 125) yielded Cronbach's α = .92 and α = .89 for the warmth/ responsiveness and structure scales respectively. A significant positive correlation between warmth/responsiveness and structure $\underline{r}$ = .65, p < .0001, N = 125), was found.

Social development

This construct was operationalized as the typical degree of warmth and task engagement (Cohn et al., 1992) that the child displayed during the play interaction with his/her mother. This construct was assessed by two three-item scales: warmth (i.e., warmth, expressiveness, and interactiveness) and task engagement (i.e., attentiveness, persistence, and planfulness). Hutcheson, Black, Talley, Dubowitz, et al. (1997) report alpha coefficients of .72 and .86 for warmth and task engagement in a sample of the same longitudinal cohort and Finn's r coefficients above .90. Analysis of the internal consistencies of these scales yielded Cronbach's α = .79 (N = 126) for warmth, and α = .78 (N = 126) for task engagement for the current sample. The intercorrelation between these two scales is $\underline{r}$ = .23, p < .009 for the current sample (N = 126).

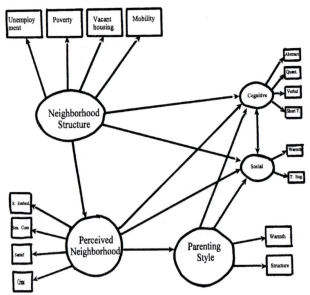

Figure 3. Initial model of hypothesized relationships among neighborhood, parenting, and development.

Cognitive development

This construct was assessed using the Stanford-Binet, Fourth Edition (Thorndike, Hagen, & Sattler, 1986). This measure has been developed and normed in nationally representative samples of children age 2–18 years and has a mean of 100 and a standard deviation of 16.

Data on two other maternal dimensions–depression and social support—that were available as part of a larger study were used in the analysis of the PNS. Depression was assessed using an adapted version of the depression section of the Diagnostic Interview Schedule (DIS-IIIR) (Robins, Helzer, Grougham, & Ratcliff, 1981). Social support was assessed by the Family Support Scale, a measure that has adequate levels of factorial, content, and criterion validity (Dunst, Jenkins, &Trivette, 1984).

DATA ANALYSES

Model specification

Figure 3 diagrams the pathways through which neighborhood characteristics are thought to influence children's social and cognitive development. Neighborhood context is posited to have two defining components—neighborhood structure (i.e., census ratings) and perceived neighborhood (i.e., maternal perceptions of neighborhood threats and resources).

For hypotheses 1a and 1b an independent model was postulated, in that structural ratings and maternal perceptions of neighborhood context at Time 3 were expected to predict cognitive and social development at Time 5.

For the second and third hypotheses, a mediator model was postulated. That is, in the second hypothesis, the influences of neighborhood structure on children's development were assumed to be indirect and to operate through maternal perceptions of the neighborhood context. For the third hypothesis, the effects of maternal perceptions of neighborhood on cognitive and social development were posited to be indirect and to operate through parenting style.

Latent variables

Because constructs such as neighborhood, parenting style, and development can not be observed but rather are inferred from certain measures, they can be treated as latent variables (Schumacker & Lomax, 1996). Often referred to as factors, latent variables are defined as the commonality among their multiple indicators (MacCallum, 1995), and are free of random error and uniqueness associated with their indicators. Five latent variables were estimated in the models fitted: neighborhood structure, perceived neighborhood, parenting style, cognitive development, and social development.

The construct of neighborhood structure was estimated through three indicators representing demographic character-istics of the neighborhood area such as poverty, unemploy-ment, and mobility (i.e., six geocode variables from the 1990 Census data). These indicators (i.e., parcels) were aimed at reducing the number of parameters to be estimated and repre-sent the mean of two or three related census ratings. For example, the indicator neighborhood poverty represented the average of the percentage of persons below the poverty level and the percentage of households with public assistance income in the census tract.

Perceived neighborhood was estimated through four dimensions of neighborhood life, as measured by the PNS: social embeddedness, sense of community, satisfaction with neighborhood, and perceived crime and signs of disorder.

Parenting style was estimated through a five-item scale of maternal warmth/responsiveness and a four-item scale of maternal structure (Cohn et al., 1992).

Cognitive development was estimated through four Stanford-Binet subscale scores (i.e., abstract reasoning, quanti-tative reasoning, verbal reasoning, and short-term memory). Social development was estimated by two scales derived from Cohn et al. (1992): (a) warmth (i.e., warmth, expressiveness, and interactiveness), and (b) task engagement (i.e., attentiveness, persistence, and planfulness) that the child displayed in interaction with his/her mother.

Model evaluation

Structural equation modeling (SEM) was used to test the fit of the proposed models to the data. SEM is a comprehensive statistical approach to testing hypotheses about relations among observed and latent variables (see Appendix 1). SEM represents a series of hypotheses about how the variables in the analysis are generated and related (Hu & Bentler, 1995). The parameters of the model are the regression coefficients and the variances and covariances of independent variables. These parameters are fundamental to interpreting the model, but they are not known and need to be estimated from the data.

SEM was selected to investigate pathways of neighborhood influences on development because it is well suited to test directional relations. Further, SEM is an appropriate method for evaluating the theory in this particular study because the hypotheses advanced involve both direct and indirect (mediating) relations.

Latent variables can be designated as either endogenous or exogenous. Within the models tested (see Fig. 3), neighborhood structure was treated as an exogenous variable. Perceived neighborhood, parenting style, cognitive, and social development were treated as endogenous variables.

Types of fit indexes

Evaluation of the fit of an SEM can refer to one of two characteristics of the model: absolute fit or incremental fit (see Appendix 1). As recommended by Hoyle and Panter (1995) results are evaluated and compared with respect to the following indices:

1. *Goodness of fit indexes.* Two omnibus indexes are reported: χ^2 and the Goodness of Fit Index (GFI). The χ^2 test assesses the magnitude of the discrepancy between the sample and fit-

ted covariance matrices. In other words, χ^2 compares the pattern of observed and estimated covariation. The parameters are estimated so that the discrepancy between the sample covariance matrix $\underline{S}$ and the implied covariance matrix $\Sigma(\theta)$ is minimal. Under an assumed distribution and the hypothesized model $\Sigma(\theta)$ for the population covariance matrix Σ , the test statistic $T = (N - 1)$ Fmin has an asymptotic (i.e., large sample) χ^2 distribution. In general, the null hypothesis $\Sigma = \Sigma (\theta)$ is rejected if the value of the T statistic exceeds a T critical value in the χ^2 distribution at an α level of significance. The T statistics derived from maximum likelihood (ML) and generalized least squares (GLS) estimation methods under the assumption of multivariate normality of variables are the most widely employed summary statistics for assessing the adequacy of an SEM. The GFI measures the relative amount of the observed variances and covariances accounted for by a model.

Sample size is a crucial factor in determining the extent to which model evaluation procedures can be trusted (Hu & Bentler, 1995). Both χ^2 and GFI are affected by sample size. With large samples, trivial differences between sample and estimated population covariances matrices are often significant (Ullman, 1996). With small samples T may not be χ^2 distributed leading to inaccurate probability levels (Hu & Bentler, 1995). Because problems associated with goodness-of-fit χ^2 tests have been recognized, other tests of model fit were also examined.

2. **Incremental fit indexes**. Three incremental fit indices are examined: two type-2 indexes (i.e., the Non-Normed Fit Index, NNFI, and the Incremental Fit Index, IFI) and one type-3 index (i.e., the Comparative Fit Index or CFI). Type-2 indexes compare the lack of fit of a target model to the lack of fit of a baseline model, usually the independence model, using the nonnegative statistic T. Values grater than .90 indicate a good fitting model. Because the NNFI (Bentler & Bonett, 1980) was generalized to all covariance matrices under various estima-

tion methods, it needs not have a 0 - 1 range (Hu & Bentler, 1995). The IFI (Bollen, 1989) was selected because it is less variable than other type-2 indexes (e.g., NNFI, Tucker-Lewis Index) and more consistent across indicators.

Type-3 indexes like the CFI, assess the relative reduction in lack of fit as estimated by the noncentral χ^2 of a target model versus a baseline model, and they vary from 0 - 1. Values grater than .90 are indicative of a good fitting model.

3. ***Degree of disconfirmability.*** This was examined by considering the root mean square error of approximation (RMSEA), which is essentially a measure of lack of fit per degree of freedom. Browne and Cudeck (1993) suggest that a RMSEA of .05 or less indicates close fit.

CHAPTER 4

Results

ANALYSIS OF THE PERCEIVED NEIGHBORHOOD SCALE

CFA was used to evaluate the adequacy of the hypothesized factor structure of the PNS at Time 3 and Time 5. Only parents who reported living in their neighborhood for at least one month were included in the analyses. Mean length of residence at Time 3 was 58.95 months (SD = 83.86) and ranged from 1- 444 months. At Time 5, the self-reported mean for length of residence was 91.87 months (SD = 122.8) and ranged from 1 - 531 months.

In order to have the same metric for all scale items, two items with a three-option format (i.e., presence of adult relatives and close friends in the neighborhood) were transformed to a five-option metric. Three dichotomous items were excluded from the analysis (i.e., one item that tapped availability of children as playmates and two items that dealt with victimization occurrences). As will be explained later, items dropped appeared not directly related to the neighborhood dimension they were intended to assess. Thus, for purposes of the analyses, the initial scale consisted of 39 items distributed as follows: 11 items for social embeddedness, 7 items for sense of community, 10 items for satisfaction with neighborhood, and 11 items for perceived crime.

As a preliminary step in the analysis, the assumption of multivariate normality required for Maximum Likelihood statistics was checked. Inspection of skewness and kurtosis estimates for each scale (i.e., social embeddedness, sense of community, satisfaction with neighborhood, and perceived crime) was carried out to detect deviations from normality. Minimal deviations from expected values were found at each point in time (see Table 3), providing support for the assumption of normally distributed variables required for subsequent analyses.

Table 3. Normality Distributions for CFA Model Variables

Variable	N		Mean		SD		Skewness		Kurtosis	
	T3	T5	T3	T5	T3	T5	T3	T5	T3	T5
S.Embeddedness	115	126	3.03	3.25	.92	.95	-.35	-.30	-.52	-.18
S.Community	115	126	3.31	3.45	.98	.92	-.27	-.41	-.58	-.42
Satisfaction	115	125	3.22	3.34	.94	.91	-.12	-.02	-.44	-.57
Perceived Crime	115	125	3.11	3.06	1.10	1.04	-.05	-.06	-.84	-.76

The aim of CFA of the PNS at Time 3 was to demonstrate that the variables chosen to reflect the latent constructs in fact did so in a statistically reliable manner. As Fig. 4 shows, the factor structure of this initial CFA was set so that each observed variable (i.e., item) was allowed to load on only one of the four latent constructs.

An initial CFA using all scale items as measured variables was fitted. Thirty nine variables (i.e., items) were used to estimate four latent factors. Models were tested using the LISREL VIII software (Jöreskog & Sörbom, 1992).

In order to set a metric for latent factors, and considering that for the purpose of this analysis it was of interest to estimate the factor variance, it was decided to fix one loading of each factor. Thus, the initial CFA model was conducted with the following specifications: (a) items were allowed to load on one latent factor, (b) factor loadings for the first item in each

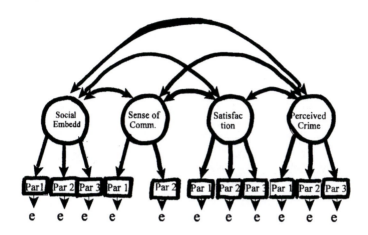

Figure 4. Hypothesized Factor Structure of the PNS

factor were fixed at 1.0, (c) factors were allowed to be correlated, and (d) errors were assumed to be uncorrelated.

This model did not adequately reflect the data as indicated by the overall fit indexes χ^2 (608, N = 110) = 1382.01, p = < .0; RMSEA = .11; GFI = .59) and a low Non- Normed Fit Index (NNFI = .69) as well as other indices of incremental fit (i.e., CFI = .72; IFI = .72) (see Table 5). The inadequate fit of this model was not surprising considering the large number of variables in the model and the small sample size. Inspection of factor loadings revealed that some items loaded on two factors therefore threatening unidimensional construct measurement.

Respecification of the initial model was done by reviewing the theoretical definition of the constructs and by examining the corresponding contents of each scale. Item analysis was conducted to examine the correlation between each item and all other items. Six items found to be insufficiently related to their scales were dropped (i.e., two items in the satisfaction scale, and four items in the crime scale). For example, close inspection of the satisfaction with neighborhood scale revealed that the scale contained items tapping different dimensions (e.g., neighborhood deterioration, desire to move from neighborhood, presence of children deemed undesirable as playmates for own children, availability of public resources, neighborhood safety) that rendered it a very heterogeneous scale. In order to obtain a more pure dimension of neighborhood satisfaction, only those items that explicitly required the respondent's cognitive-affective assessment of the neighborhood physical environment (Ringel & Finkelstein, 1991) and the respondent's assessment of the resources available to raise children (Coulton et al., 1996) were retained.

A similar situation was observed in the perceived crime scale. In order to obtain a shorter scale that would reflect a conceptually purer fear of crime factor, only items that measured threat of crime and presence of social and physical incivilities were retained.

In order to reduce the number of parameters to be estimated in the measurement model, and in search of more stable estimates given the small sample size (Anderson & Gerbing, 1988; Hoyle, 1995) and the excessive number of items in each scale, item parcels were developed to reflect each factor of the PNS. Item parcels are a commonly used method of reexpression of variables, by summing or taking the mean of several items that purportedly measure the same construct. Parcels typically exhibit distributions that more closely approach a normal distribution than the original items (West, Finch, & Curran, 1995).

Parcels were construed by taking the mean of two or three related items. Scale items were grouped into parcels based on the correlations among them. Thus, the use of item parcels was expected to eliminate redundancy in the model and to add parsimony to the parameter estimates.

The latent construct of perceived neighborhood was reflected in 11 indicators that reflect social embeddedness (three-item parcels), sense of community (one four-item and one three-item parcel), satisfaction with neighborhood (three-item parcels), and perceived crime (two three-item and one two-item parcel).

A second CFA was fitted for the Time 3 data with the same specifications as the initial CFA (i.e., item parcels were allowed to load on one latent factor, factor loadings for the first item parcel in each factor were fixed at 1.0, and factors were allowed to be correlated). This model reflected the data better as indicated by the significant loadings of item parcels on their respective factors. Unstandardized values for all loadings were above the critical ratio of 1.96. Table 4 presents the standardized values. Both the overall χ^2 (38, N = 114) = 52.08, p = < .064; RMSEA = .06, (p value for the test of close fit = .36); GFI = .93, and the incremental indexes (i.e., NNFI = .97, IFI = .98, and CFI = .98) indicated adequate fit of the model.

A subsequent CFA model with the same specifications was performed on the Time 5 data. Again, the results of this analysis yielded significant loadings of indicators on their respective factors (see Table 4), and adequate indices of comparative fit (i.e., NNFI = .94; IFI = .96, and CFI = .96). However, compared to the Time 3 model values (see Table 5), the overall fit of the Time 5 model to the data was poorer χ^2 (38, N =125) = 81.80, p = < .001; RMSEA = .08 (p value for test of close fit of .044), and a GFI = .91. Interfactor correlations for the final CFA models are presented in Tables 6 and 7.

Inspection of the matrix of loadings of measured variables on latent constructs indicated that the first parcel (i.e., perception of safety to walk at night, evidence of public drinking and drug use/dealing) and the second parcel (i.e., fear of being killed, mugged, or raped) of perceived crime loaded high on neighborhood satisfaction as well, indicating that there is shared variance between these two factors, possibly method variance. A second version of the Time 5 model was fitted, this time allowing errors of all perceived crime parcels to be correlated with errors of the first two satisfaction parcels. The overall fit of this model improved as indicated by the omnibus test χ^2 (32, N = 125) = 58.79, p = < .002; RMSEA = .08 (p value for test of close fit = .06); GFI = .92, and the incremental fit indexes (i.e., NNFI = .94; CFI = .97; IFI = .97).

*Table 4. Factor Structure, Standardized Loadings and
Reliabilities of the PNS at Two Points in Time*

Factor	Loadings		Loadings	
Social Embeddedness		.80		.83
Parcel 1 Participate neighborhood activities Visit with neighbors Get help from neighbors	.95		.90	
Parcel 2 Loan money/food from neighbor Borrow money/food from neighbor Give help to neighbor	.87		.90	
Parcel 3 Greet neighbor Talk to neighbors/parents Exchange child care	.68		.67	
Sense of Community		.86		.85
Parcel 1 Feel belong in neighborhood Feel close to neighbors People trust each other	1.02		.94	
Parcel 2 Look out for one another Rely on neighbors Care what neighbors think People usually warm	.83		.77	
Satisfaction with Neighborhood		.86		.83
Parcel 1 Good place to live; Good place to raise family Access to telephone	.92		.82	
Parcel 2 Good place for children to play Safe for child to play outside Access to transportation	.62		.65	
Parcel 3 Buildings/yard run down; Move out if could Neighborhood getting worse	.89		.88	
Perceived Crime		.91		.85
Parcel 1 Open drug use/dealing; Public drinking Safe to walk at night	.86		.86	
Parcel 2 Afraid being mugged; Afraid being raped Afraid being killed	.99		.82	
Parcel 3 Afraid being robbed; Friends/relatives don't vist Troublemakers hanging around	.97		.76	

In summary, the results of the analyses described above provide support for the four- factor structure of the PNS, at two points in time. These factors (i.e., social embeddedness, sense of community, satisfaction with neighborhood, and perceived crime) are consistent with the four dimensions derived from the literature review and were included in the models for subsequent hypotheses testing.

Reliability

Because the PNS scale was newly created, its reliability as a measure of individual perceptions was also examined. Coefficient α was calculated to estimate the internal consistency of each scale, based on the composite score for the item parcels, at each point in time.

Table 4 presents reliabilities for the PNS factors at Time 3 and Time 5. As can be seen, α coefficients are above .80 for all scales, ranging from .80 to .91 for the Time 3 and from .83 to .85 for the Time 5 scales. Within each scale, α coefficients are very similar across occasions. Overall, internal consistencies (i.e., as indicated by Cronbach's alpha) for each PNS scale factor are consistent from Time 3 to Time 5.

Table 5. *Summary of Model Fit Indices for Confirmatory Factor Analysis of the PNS Scale*

Model	χ^2	*df*	*p*	GFI	NNFI
Initial CFA T3	1382.01	608	.0	.59	.69
Initial CFA T3	52.08	38	.06	.93	.97
Initial CFA T3	81.80	38	.00	.91	.94
Initial CFA T3	58.79	32	.002	.92	.94

Table 6. *PNS Inter-factor Correlations at Time 3*

	S.Embeddedness	S.Community	Satisfaction
S.Embeddedness			
S.Community	.80***		
Satisfaction	.28**	.69***	
Perceived Crime	-.10	-.47***	-.80***

*p<.05; **p<.01; ***p<.001

Table 7. *PNS Inter-factor Correlations at Time 5*

	S.Embeddedness	S.Community	Satisfaction
S.Embeddedness			
S.Community	.65***		
Satisfaction	.03	.56***	
Perceived Crime	.02	-.41***	-.82***

*p<.05; **p<.01; ***p<.001

Evidence for Construct Validity

The finding that each indicator's estimated pattern coefficient (see Table 4) on its posited underlying construct is significant provides evidence for convergent validity (Anderson & Gerbing, 1988). Both at Time 3 and Time 5, the pattern of loadings of indicators on the hypothesized constructs was in the expected direction.

Additional evidence for construct validity was obtained from correlational analyses between census ratings of neighborhood and PNS subscales. There was a significant negative correlation between neighborhood poverty and satisfaction with neighborhood both at Time 3 r = -.35, p < .0002; N = 115) and Time 5 (r = - .44, p < .0001; N = 125). Similarly, neighborhood poverty was significantly correlated with perceptions of crime both at Time 3(r = .31, p < .007; N = 115) and Time 5 (r = .39, p < .00; N = 125) indicating that signs of neighborhood poverty are associated with signs of community disorder. Overall, these correlations are in the expected direction.

A significant positive correlation was found between mothers' desire to move out of the neighborhood and perception of crime both at Time 3 (r = .60, p < .0001; N = 115) and Time 5 (r = .66, p < .0001; N = 125). Similarly, significant positive correlations were found between perception of crime and neighborhood deterioration at Time 3 (r = .51, p < .0001; N= 115) and Time 5 (r = .49, p < .0001; N = 125). However, no significant correlations between perception of crime and participation in neighborhood activities were found for Time 3 (r = .01, p < .90; N = 115) and Time 5 (r = .08, p < .34; N = 125). The latter suggests that actual and perceived measures of crime do not necessarily reduce social involvement in the neighborhood.

There was no significant correlation between neighborhood mobility (i.e., percentage of people who move out of neighborhood, percentage of housing units vacant) and social embeddedness at Time 3 (r = -.16, p < .09; N = 115) or Time 5 (r = -.08, p < .38; N = 115). Similarly, no significant correlations were found between mobility and satisfaction with neighborhood (r = -.10, p < .26; N = 115 for Time 3 and r = -.11, p < .23, N = 125 for Time 5) and between mobility and perceived crime (r = .07, p < .42; N = 115 for Time 3 and r = -.02, p < .79, N = 125 for Time 5). As for mothers' perception of sense of community, a significant negative correlation was found with mobility at Time 5 (r = -.21, p < .02; N = 126) but not at Time 3 (r = -.14, p < .13; N = 115).

Correlations Among PNS Scales and Other Psychological Dimensions

As expected, correlational analyses indicated that length of residence in the neighborhood at Time 3 was positively associated with social embeddedness (r = .26; p < .005; N = 114) and sense of community (r = .21; p < .03; N = 114) at Time 3.

However, at Time 5, length of residence in the neighborhood was neither associated with sense of community (r = .16; p < .07; N = 126) nor with social embeddedness (r = .08; p < .41; N = 126). Similarly, length of residence at Time 3 and Time 5 was not significantly related to either satisfaction with neighborhood (r = - .04; p < .70; N = 114 and (r = .02; p < .82; N = 125 respectively) or perception of crime (r = - .01; p < .93; N = 114 and r = .03; p < .76; N = 125 respectively).

Consistent with expectations, significant positive correlations between social support and social embeddedness in the neighborhood at Time 3 and Time 5 (r = .25, p < .009; N = 111, and r = .29; p < .001; N = 123, respectively) were found. Similarly, significant positive correlations between social support and sense of community were found for both Time 3 and Time 5 (r = .26; p < .006; N = 111, and r = .32; p < .0003; N = 123, respectively), and between social support and satisfaction with neighborhood at Time 3 (r = .19; p < .05; N = 111). Looking at specific sources of social support, significant positive correlations between informal kinship support and social embeddedness (r = .22; p < .03; N = 98) and sense of community (r = .35; p < .0004; N = 98), and a significant negative correlation with perceived crime (r = -.22; p < .03; N = 98) were found at Time 5.

Significant negative correlations were found between maternal depression and perceptions of sense of community (r = -.19; p < .04; N = 115) and, between maternal depression and satisfaction with neighborhood (r = -.18; p < .05; N = 115) at Time 3. As expected, a significant positive correlation between maternal depression and fear of crime (r = .21, p < .02; N = 115) was found at Time 3.

A significant negative correlation between social support and perceived crime (r = - .21; p < .02; N = 111) was found at Time 3 but not at Time 5 (r = -.16; p < .08; N = 122). At Time 5 significant positive correlations between social support and social embeddedness (r = .29, p < .001; N = 123), sense of community (r = .32; p < .0003; N = 123), and satisfaction with neighborhood (r = .28; p < .001; N = 122) were found.

Stability of the PNS Scale Scores From Time 3 to Time 5

Pearson correlations between Time 3 and Time 5 scores for each of the PNS factors were calculated for the group that did not move (n = 87). As can be seen from Table 8, results indicated significant positive correlations of similar magnitude between the Time 3 and Time 5 social embeddedness ($\underline{r}$ = .51; p < .0001; n = 86), sense of community ($\underline{r}$ = .53; p < .0001; n = 86), and perceived crime ($\underline{r}$ = .46; p < .0001; n = 86) factors. Scores on the satisfaction with neighborhood scale were not significantly related from Time 3 to Time 5 ($\underline{r}$ = .18, p < .10; n = 86).

A one-way Anova examined differences in Time 3 and Time 5 PNS scale scores by comparing mothers who moved with those who did not. As shown in Table 9, findings indicated no significant differences between Time 3 and Time 5 PNS scores for mothers who remained in the same neighborhood (n = 86) in the social embeddedness (df = 1, MS = .51, F =.50, p = .48), sense of community (df = 1, MS = .25, F = .25, p = .62), satisfaction with neighborhood (df = 1, MS = .04, F = .03, p = .87), and fear of crime (df = 1, MS =.05, F = .05, p = .82) scales. In other words, mean scores for the PNS scales were stable over the two-year period in the current sample.

Examination of correlations between scale scores at Time 3 and Time 5 indicated moderate to high stability (i.e., range .46 to .53) in maternal perceptions of social embeddedness, sense of community and perceived crime for mothers who did not move. However, a low correlation between the satisfaction with neighborhood scores at Time 3 and Time 5 was found. This finding suggests that maternal satisfaction with neighborhood may change as children grow and needs change.

Table 8. *Pearson Correlation Coefficients Between T3 and T5 PNS Factor Scores for the Group That Did Not Move*

	1	2	3	4	5	6	7
1. Social embeddedness T3							
2. Sense community T3	.64***						
3. Satisfaction T3	.28***	.57***					
4. Perceived crime T3	-.10	-.36***	-.69***				
5. Social embeddedness T5	.51***						
6. Sense community T5		.53			.51***		
7. Satisfaction T5			.18		-.03	-.36	
8. Perceived crime T5				.46*** .14		-.24	-.67***

$*p<.05;$ $**p<.01;$ $***p<.001$

Table 9. *Differences in the PNS Scale Scores From Time 3 to Time 5 For the Group That Did Not Move*

	N	Mean	S.Error	t	p
Social embeddedness	86	0.19	0.10	1.89	0.06
Sense community	86	0.08	0.10	0.85	0.40
Satisfaction	86	0.12	0.11	0.97	0.33
Perceived crime	86	0.09	0.11	-0.85	0.40

Selection Bias

Available data for the current study allow neither assessment nor modeling of the non-random selection processes that bring together individuals with particular socioeconomic characteristics and behavioral dispositions within neighborhoods. In order to account for selection effects (i.e., whether families who moved were different from those who did not move) several statistical tests were performed to compare families who moved with those who did not on demographic characteristics such as education, occupation, marital status, and type of housing.

Analysis of variance examined differences in maternal education between families who moved (n = 32) and those who did not move (n = 87) from Time 3 to Time 5. Results indicated no significant differences between groups for maternal education (df = 1, MS = 1.9; F = .95, p < 0.33) and maternal age (df = 1, MS = 17.38; F = .53, p < 0.47). Chi square analyses were used to examine other demographic differences between mothers who moved and those who did not. Findings indicated no significant differences between groups in marital status (df = 1, χ^2 = .31, p < .58; N = 129), maternal employment status (df = 1, χ^2 = 1.13, p < .29; N = 129), single-parent status (df = 1, χ^2 = 3.60, p < .06; N = 129), or type of housing (df = 1, χ^2 = .09, p < .76; N = 127).

Additional analyses compared mothers who reported a desire to move out of the neighborhood (n = 64) to those who reported no desire to move (n = 65) at Time 3. Findings indicated no significant group differences for maternal education (df = 1, MS = 4.51; F = 2.28, p < 0.13) and maternal age (df = 1, MS = 36.85; F = 1.14, p < 0.29), marital status (df = 1, χ^2 = 2.14, p < 1.43; N = 129), maternal employment status (df = 1, χ^2 = .42, p < .52; n=129), or single-parent status (df = 1, χ^2 = .47, p < .49; N = 129). However, a significant difference was found for type of housing (df = 1, χ^2 = 12.19, p < .001; N = 127), indicating that mothers living in public housing at Time 3 more frequently reported a desire to move.

A nonsignificant correlation between mothers reporting a desire to move out of the neighborhood at Time 3 and actual move at Time 4 was found. Although no definite conclusions regarding selection effects operating within neighborhoods can be drawn, the results described above indicate that families who moved, and families who report a desire to move are comparable to those who did not move and to those who do not desire to move on most demographic characteristics.

HYPOTHESIS TESTING

Model Variables

Prior to hypotheses testing, the assumption of multivariate normality was checked by examining the departure from normality for each model variable. Inspection of Table 10 indicates that with the exception of the parental structure and the child warmth and task engagement scales, the distributions of model variables minimally depart from normality.

Perceived neighborhood

As described earlier, the latent construct of perceived neighborhood was reflected in four multi-item indicators assessed at Time 3 and at Time 5. The items are described in Table 4. For each respondent, scores on each of the four subscales (i.e., social embeddedness, sense of community, satisfaction with neighborhood, and fear of crime) of the PNS were calculated. Subscale scores were calculated by adding the score on the individual items and dividing by the number of items.

Parenting style

Repeated measures Anova performed on the warmth and structure scales at three points in time (Time 3, Time 4, and Time 5) yielded no significant differences in levels of parental warmth (df= 2, $F = 1.42$, $p < .25$), and parental structure (df = 2, $F = 1.91$, $p < .15$) between occasions. Univariate contrasts yielded no significant differences between occasions for parental warmth (i.e., df = 1, MS = 0.09, $F = 0.21$, $p < 0.65$ for Time 3 and Time 4 warmth; df = 1, MS = 0.47, $F = 1.98$, $p < .16$ for Time 3 and Time 5 warmth; and df = 1, MS = 0.95, $F = 2.11$, $p < .15$ for Time 4 and Time 5 warmth). Similarly, univariate contrasts for parental structure indicated no significant differences between occasions (i.e., df = 1, MS = 1, $F = 0.21$, $p < .65$ for Time 3 and Time 4 structure; df = 1, MS = 1.15, $F = 2.07$, $p < .15$ for Time 3 and Time 5 structure; and df = 1, MS = 1.15, $F = 3.34$, $p < .007$ for Time 4 and Time 5 structure).

Table 10. *Means, Standard Deviations, Skewness, and Kurtosis for Variables in Longitudinal Models*

	N	Mean	SD	Skewness	Kurtosis
Rental/vacant housing	129	0.63	0.18	-.56	.43
Poverty	126	0.34	0.15	.26	-.07
Unemployment	126	0.17	0.07	.57	.37
S.Embedded.	115	3.22	0.93	-.19	-.52
S.Community	115	3.31	0.98	-.27	-.58
Satisfaction	115	3.22	0.93	-.12	-.43
Crime	115	3.07	1.07	.13	-.66
Par. warmth	125	2.90	0.62	-.14	.15
Par. structure	125	2.90	0.68	.12	-.80
Abstract	124	81.88	12.18	.05	-.47
Quantitative	120	95.70	10.52	-.64	.41
Short term	123	88.41	10.40	.14	.26
Verbal	124	91.94	11.93	-.57	-.08
Child warmth	126	2.87	0.51	-.60	1.80
T. engagement	126	2.92	0.39	-1.53	6.76

Given that no significant differences between waves were found for parenting style (i.e., scores on the warmth/responsiveness and structure scales), this latent factor was represented by the Time 4 data in the longitudinal models. The Time 4 wave was considered a representative indicator of parenting style (i.e., a midpoint in time span of the study) and consisted of observations collected one year before the outcome measures.

Cognitive development

As mentioned earlier, cognitive development was estimated by four indicators representing scores on each of the Stanford Binet Intelligence Scale areas: abstract reasoning, quantitative reasoning, verbal reasoning, and short-term memory.

Respecification of indicators for latent constructs

After examining the patterns of loadings of measured variables on latent factors, and the squared multiple correlations, it became apparent that mobility did not load significantly on neighborhood structure and did not add significantly to the factor beyond the contribution of neighborhood poverty, unemployment, and housing. Similarly, the parental structure scale did not load significantly on parenting. Based on the above observations and in search of a more parsimonious solution, the decision was made to drop the mobility ratings from the neighborhood structure factor, and the structure scale from the parenting style factor.

Control for Demographic Differences

To reduce the potential confound of maternal education and to prevent distortions in the associations between neighborhood characteristics and social and cognitive development, this variable was included in all models fitted. Maternal education was treated as a measured variable. The regression coefficients representing the direct effects of maternal education on development were estimated. In all models tested, maternal education was allowed to correlate with neighborhood structure.

Longitudinal Models

The independent and mediator models for the interrelationships among neighborhood characteristics and developmental outcomes were tested using the LISREL VIII software. The longitudinal models at Time 5 included 19 measured variables to estimate 5 latent factors (i.e., neighborhood structure, perceived neighborhood, parental warmth, and child cognitive and social development) and maternal education as a measured variable. Appendix 2 presents the correlation matrix for the variables in the model.

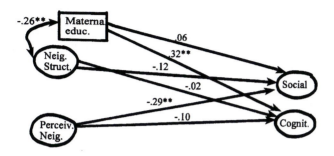

Figure 5. Longitudinal model of direct effects of neighborhood on child development

X^2 (84, N =99) =187.12 p ~ 0
RMSEA=.11
GFI=.81
NNFI=.77

Model for hypotheses 1a and 1b

A longitudinal model tested the relationships between neighborhood variables at Time 3 and child cognitive and social development at Time 5, controlling for maternal education. Only direct effects of neighborhood structure and perceived neighborhood on cognitive and social development were tested in the first model. This model was fitted with the following specifications: (a) loadings for the first item of each latent factor were set at 1, to establish a metric for the latent factor. Loadings for the rest of the items were freely estimated; (b) variances for all latent factors were freely estimated; (c) covariation between the disturbance terms of each outcome measure (i.e., social and cognitive development) was freely estimated; (d) only error variances of observed variables were estimated and error terms were not allowed to be correlated, (e) regression coefficients representing the direct effects of maternal education on cognitive and social development were estimated, and (f) maternal education was allowed to correlate with neighborhood structure.

Results of this model yielded significant loadings of all indicators on their corresponding latent factors. However, the overall fit of the model was poor. The χ^2 (84, N = 99) = 187.12 was significant (p = < .00), the RMSEA was fairly large (.11), and the GFI was low (.81).

The incremental fit indices were fairly small (i.e., NNFI = .77, CFI = .82, and IFI = .82) indicating poor fit as well. Examination of beta coefficients (see Fig. 5 for standardized coefficients) indicated no significant pathways from neighborhood structure to either cognitive (β = -.01, std. error = .06, t = -.22) or social (β = -.97, std. error = .82, t = -.1.17) development. Thus, no support was provided for hypothesis 1a, namely that significant covariation between neighborhood structure and child development would be found. However, a significant effect of maternal education on cognitive development was found (β = .02, std. error = .006, t = 2.62).

Additionally, a significant effect of perceived neighborhood on social development was found (β = -.49, std. error = .20, t = -2.42), thus providing partial support for hypothesis 1b (i.e., that perceived neighborhood would have a direct effect on development). No significant effects of perceived neighborhood on cognitive development were found (β = -.01, std. error = .013, t = -.92).

Examination of the squared multiple correlations indicated that maternal education and the neighborhood variables accounted for 12.00 % of the variance in cognitive development, and for 10.63 % of the variance in social development.

Models for Hypothesis 2 and 3

A variable functions as a mediator when it accounts for the relation between a predictor and the criterion. According to Baron and Kenny (1986), criteria for testing mediation are: (a) variations in levels of neighborhood structure significantly account for variations in perceived neighborhood (i.e., path a); (b) variations in perceived neighborhood (mediator) significantly account for variations in child development (i.e., path b); and (c) if paths a and b are controlled, a previously significant relation between neighborhood structure and child development is no longer significant, with the strongest demonstration of significance occurring when path c is 0. The mediator model postulated for Hypothesis 2 was to be assessed using the Baron and Kenny (1986) criteria by comparing the association between structure neighborhood and child development with and without perceived neighborhood and evaluating the fit of each of these models.

A saturated model examined nine pathways of both direct and indirect effects of neighborhood structure and perceived neighborhood on social and cognitive development (see Fig. 6). The saturated model tested all direct and indirect effects of neighborhood structure and perceived neighborhood on development. The overall fit of this model was not adequate as indicated by a significant χ^2 (158, N = 99) = 236.74, p = < .00005; RMSEA = .007, (p value for test of close fit of .04), and a GFI = .82. Again, examination of the pattern of loadings revealed that all indicators had significant loadings on their corresponding latent factors, and the incremental fit indexes were sufficiently large (i.e., NNFI = .90, IFI = .92, and CFI = .91) to suggest that minor modifications to the model could yield a better fit.

Consistent with results from the model for Hypothesis 1a and 1b, no significant pathways from neighborhood structure to either cognitive (β = -.02, std. error = .06, t = - .36) or social (β = -.27, std. error = .29, t = -.92) development were found (see Fig. 6 for standardized coefficients). Two pathways were significant: (a) a negative effect of perceived neighborhood on social development (β = -.17, std. error = .07, t = -2.37), and (b) a positive effect of maternal education on cognitive development were found (β = .02, std. error = .006, t = 2.60). Again, nosignificant effects of perceived neighborhood on cognitive development were found (β = -.01, std. error = .013, t = -.92).

Examination of the squared multiple correlations indicated that the overall model accounted for 12.03 % of the variance in cognitive development, and for 10.10 % of the variance in social development.

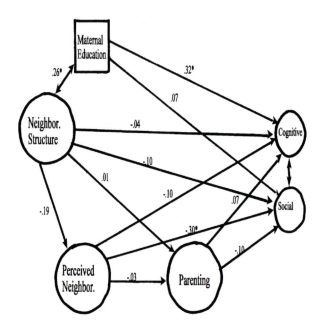

X^2 (158, N=99)=236.74, p=.00005
RMSEA= .07
GFI= .82
NNFI= .90

Figure 6. Longitudinal saturated model

The results reported above provided confirmation for the second criterion for testing the mediational effect of perceived neighborhood on child development, namely that variations in perceived neighborhood significantly account for variations in social development. However, no significant beta weights were found for the pathway between neighborhood structure and social development. Therefore, Hypothesis 2 could not be tested as originally proposed.

A similar situation prevented testing Hypothesis 3, namely that parenting style mediates the effects of perceived neigh-

borhood on child development. Although the first criterion
for mediation was met (i.e., namely that perceived neighborhood has a direct effect on social development), no significant
effects of parenting style on either cognitive (β = .01, std. error
= .017, t = .60) or social (β = -.08, std. error = .090, t = -.90)
development were found.

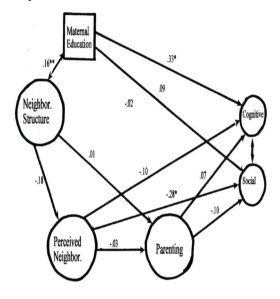

X^2 (160, N=99)= 237.58 (p=.0000)
RMSEA=.07
GFI= .82
NNFI= .90

Figure 7. Longitudinal reduced 1 model

An alternative—sequential—approach was taken to test
the direct and indirect effects of neighborhood structure, perceived neighborhood, and parenting on child development.
For this purpose the fit of three nested models was compared
and tested for χ^2 differences. The first model—saturated—is

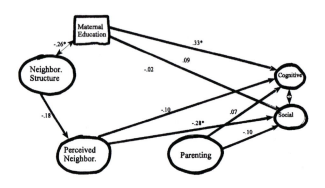

X^2 (162, N=99)= 237.67 (p=.0000)
RMSEA=.07
GFI= .82
NNFI= .90

Figure 8. Longitudinal reduced 2 model

equivalent to the model fitted for Hypotheses 2 and 3. In the second model, direct pathways from neighborhood structure to cognitive and social development were eliminated (see Fig. 7). These paths had non-significant beta coefficients in the saturated version of the model. Results of this more parsimonious model yielded an overall fit χ^2 (160, N = 99,) = 237.58, p = < .0000; RMSEA = .07 (p value for test of close fit of .45); GFI = .82. The incremental fit indexes indicated better fit than the omnibus tests (i.e., NNFI = .90, IFI = .92, and CFI = .91). Examination of beta coefficients (see Fig. 7 for standardized coefficients) indicated that the pathway from neighborhood structure to perceived neighborhood was in the expected direction but not significant (β = -.85, std. error = .47, t = -1.81). The pathway from perceived neighborhood to social development continued to be significant (β = -.17, std. error = .07, t = -2.29). The difference in χ^2 values between the saturated and the second model was not significant ($\Delta\chi^2$ =.83, df = 2, p > .05), providing support for the more parsimonious model. However, no support for the indirect effects of neighborhood structure (i.e., through maternal perceptions of neighborhood) on child development was provided because there was no significant direct effect of neighborhood structure on outcome.

Finally, in a more parsimonious model direct pathways from neighborhood structure to parenting and from perceived neighborhood to parenting were eliminated (see Fig. 8). Neither of these paths were significant in the previous model. As expected, this model yielded a slightly poorer overall fit χ^2 (162, N = 99) = 237.67, p = < .0001; RMSEA = .07 (p value for test of close fit = .05) and a GFI = .82. However, the incremental fit indexes were improved (i.e., NNFI = .93, IFI = .95, and CFI = .95). Examination of beta coefficients (Fig. 8 presents standardized coefficients) indicated that the pathway from perceived neighborhood to social development continued to be significant (β = -.17, std. error = .07, t = -2.30). As Table 11 shows, the difference in χ^2 values between the third and the second model is not significant ($\Delta\chi^2$ = .10, df = 2, p > .05), providing support for the more parsimonious model. However, no support for the indirect effects of perceived neighborhood (i.e., through parenting) on child development was provided because there was no significant direct effect of the mediator on outcome. This final model accounted for 11.9 % of the variance in cognitive development, and for 9.5 % of the variance in social development.

Table 11. *Summary Fit Indices for Nested Sequence of Longitudinal Models*

Model	χ^2	df	GFI	NNFI	χ^2 diff.	df diff.
Direct effects only	187.12	84	.81	.77		
Saturated	236.74	158	.82	.90		
Reduced 1	237.58	160	.82	.90	.83	2
Reduced 2	237.67	162	.86	.90	.10	2

*p<.05

Cross-sectional Models at Time 5

The model of linear relationships between neighborhood characteristics and child development was tested cross-sectionally in a sample of 170 African American mothers and their children. This sample was extracted from the same population as the longitudinal sample and was comparable to the longitudinal sample in some demographic characteristics such as education, marital status, and single parenting status. However, mothers in this sample had lower levels of unemployment (56.3 %). As in the longitudinal sample, children were predominantly female (54.0 %) (see Table 12).

The data for all variables in this model—except census ratings—were collected at Time 5. Table 13 depicts means and standard deviations for all variables in the models. The correlation matrix is presented in Appendix 3.

The cross-sectional models at Time 5 included 19 measured variables to estimate five latent factors (i.e., neighborhood structure, perceived neighborhood, parental warmth, cognitive, and social development) and maternal education as a measured variable.

The first model examined only direct pathways from neighborhood structure and perceived neighborhood to social and cognitive development (see Fig. 9).

This model was fitted with the following specifications: (a) loadings for the first item of each latent factor were set at 1, to set a metric for the latent factor. Loadings for the rest of the items were freely estimated; (b) variances for all latent factors were freely estimated; (c) covariation between the disturbance terms of each outcome measure (i.e., social and cognitive development) was freely estimated; (d) only error variances of observed variables were estimated and error terms were not allowed to be correlated, (e) regression coefficients representing the direct effects of maternal education on cognitive and social development were estimated, and (f) maternal education was allowed to correlate with neighborhood structure.

Table 12. Descriptive Characteristics of Sample for T5 Cross-sectional Models

Model	Mean	SD	Range
Characteristics of Mothers			
Education (in years)	11.5	1/5	6.0–15.0
Martial status: single	64.4[a]		
Public Assistance			
Medical assistance	78.8[a]		
AFDC	68.2[a]		
Single parents	84.2[a]		
Characteristics of Children			
Age (in months)	61.2	2.09	56.0–68.0
Gender			
Males	46.0[a]		
Females	54.0[a]		
Race			
African American	100.0[a]		

[a] Expressed as percentage

Table 13. Means, Standard Deviations, Skewness, and Kurtosis for Variables in Cross-sectional Models

	N	Mean	SD	Skewness	Kurtosis
Rental/vacant housing	206	0.62	0.18	-.22	-.18
Poverty	206	0.33	0.17	.33	-.34
Unemployment	206	0.17	0.08	-.60	.20
S.Embedded.	202	3.21	0.90	-.15	-.34
S.Community	202	3.48	0.94	-.40	-.46
Satisfaction	115	3.22	0.93	-.12	-.43
Crime	115	3.07	1.07	.13	-.66
Par. warmth	125	2.90	0.62	-.14	.15
Abstract	124	81.88	12.18	.05	-.47
Quantitative	120	95.70	10.52	-.64	.41
Short memory	122	88.41	10.40	.14	.26
Verbal	124	91.94	11.93	-.57	-.08
Child warmth	126	2.87	0.51	-.60	1.80

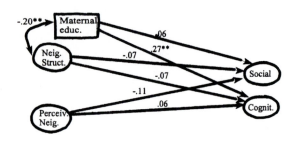

X² (84, N =159) =288.55 p ~ 0
RMSEA=.12
GFI=.82
NNFI=.71

Figure 9. Cross-sectional model of direct effects of neighborhood on child development

Results of the above model yielded an overall fit of χ^2 (84, N = 159) = 288.55, p < .0, RMSEA = .12, GFI = .82. The incremental indices indicated poor fit as well (NNFI = .71, CFI = .76, and IFI = .77). A significant effect of maternal education on cognitive development was found (β = .01, std. error = .004, t = 2.86). No significant effects of neighborhood structure on either cognitive (β = -.04, std. error = .05, t = -.89) or social (β = -.50, std. error = .57, t = -.87) development were found. Similarly, the pathways from perceived neighborhood to cognitive and social development were not significant (β = .01, std. error = .011, t = .87 and β = -.25, std. error = .15, t = .1.69, respectively). Overall, the neighborhood and maternal education factors together predicted 9.0 % and 2.1 % of the variance in cognitive and social development respectively.

Unfortunately, because no significant effects of neighborhood structure on either cognitive or social development were observed, no further tests of the mediating effects of perceived neighborhood on development could be done cross-sectionally. Similarly, because no significant effects of perceived neighborhood on social development were found, no further test of Hypothesis 3 (i.e. mediational effects of parenting on development) could be done cross-sectionally.

Alternatively, a sequence of nested models tested the direct and indirect effects of neighborhood structure, perceived neighborhood, and parenting on child development. For this purpose the fit of three nested models was compared and tested for chi square differences.

The saturated version of this model examined nine pathways of both direct and indirect effects of neighborhood structure and perceived neighborhood on social and cognitive development. Results of this model yielded an overall fit of χ^2 (158, N = 159) = 287.00, p < .00, RMSEA = .07. The GFI = .86. Though two incremental indexes (i.e., CFI = .91, and IFI = .91) suggested acceptable fit, the model had some problems. Not only was the χ^2 significant, but the RMSEA and the NNFI (i.e., .89) were not optimal. Inspection of the pattern of loadings of measured variables on their corresponding constructs revealed significant loadings for all indicators except for those of perceived neighborhood. The latter had very large standard errors suggesting estimation problems. No significant pathways between neighborhood factors and child development were found. Two pathways were significant: (a) a positive effect of maternal education on cognitive development (β = .01, std. error = .005, t = 2.7), and (b) a significant positive relationship between parental warmth and social development (β = .56, std. error = .11, t = 4.90).

Results from the above model suggested two issues to be addressed in model respecification. First, examination of modification indices for each parameter of the model indicated common variance (i.e., indicators tended to load on both factors) between social embeddedness and sense of community. To prevent capitalizing on chance by correlating errors of these two indicators (Anderson & Gerbing, 1988), the decision was made to drop the social embeddedness indicators from the perceived neighborhood construct. Second, to rule out the possibility that the significance of the pathway between parental warmth and child warmth was due to method variance, correlations between the parenting and child warmth residuals (i.e., correlated errors) were included in subsequent versions of this model.

Thus, a second cross-sectional model including 18 measured variables to estimate the same five latent factors was fitted. Again, the saturated version of this model examined direct and indirect effects of neighborhood structure and perceived neighborhood on social and cognitive development and was fitted with the same specifications described above. This model had a better fit as indicated by a pattern of significant loadings of each indicator on their corresponding latent factors. As can be seen in Table 13, the overall fit of the model was χ^2 (125, N = 159) = 193.14, p < .00008, RMSEA = .06 (p value for test of close fit = .18). The GFI = .89.

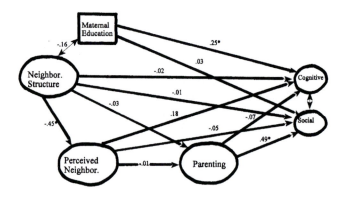

Figure 10. Cross-sectional saturated model

X^2 (125, N=159)= 193.14
(p=.0000)
RMSEA=.06
GFI= .89
NNFI= .93

Although the χ^2 was significant, the incremental indexes were sufficiently large to indicate a better fit (i.e., NNFI = .93, CFI = .95, and IFI = .95). Three pathways were significant (Fig. 10 presents standardized coefficients): (a) a significant negative relationship between neighborhood structure and perceived

neighborhood was found (β = - 1.33, std. error = .34, t = - 3.88),
(b) a significant positive relationship between parental
warmth and social development was found (β = .55, std. error
= .12, t = 4.55), and (c) a significant positive relationship
between maternal education and cognitive development (β =
.01, std. error = .005, t = 2.67) was found.

The relationship between perceived neighborhood and
cognitive development was in the expected direction but not
significant (β = .03, std. error = .02, t = 1.58). Overall, the
neighborhood and parenting factors together predicted 11.42
% and 24.63 % of the variance in cognitive and social development respectively.

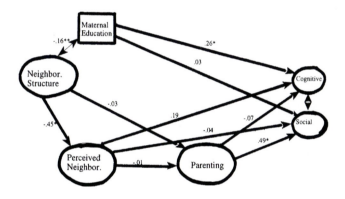

Figure 11. Cross-sectional reduced 1 model

X^2 (127, N=159)= 193.20
(p =.0001)
RMSEA=.06
GFI= .89
NNFI= .93

Alternatively, two more parsimonious models were fitted
and chi square differences between these nested models were
examined. As can be seen in Fig. 11, in the first reduced
model direct paths from neighborhood structure to cognitive
and social development were eliminated. As expected, this
reduced model yielded a larger χ^2 (127, N = 159) = 193.20, p <

.0001, RMSEA = .06 (p value for test of close fit = .22). The GFI
for this model was .89. However, the difference in χ² values
between this reduced and the saturated model was not significant (Δχ² = .06 , df = 2, p > .05), providing support for the more
parsimonious model. The regression coefficients for the pathways from neighborhood structure to perceived neighborhood
(β = -1.33, std.error = .34, t = - 3.89), and from parenting style
to social development (β = .55, std.error = .12, t = 4.55) continued to be significant in this model.

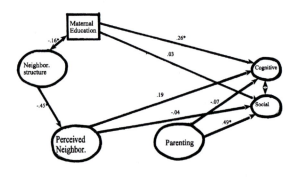

Figure12. Cross-sectional reduced 2 model

X² (129, N=159= 193.29 (p.=.000)
RMSEA=.06
GFI= .89
NNFI= .94

Finally, an even more parsimonious model was tested.
This further reduced model was fitted eliminating paths that
were close to zero, namely from neighborhood structure to
parenting and from perceived neighborhood to parenting (see
Fig. 12). The overall fit of this model yielded a χ² (129, N =
159) = 193.30, p < .0002, RMSEA = .05 (p value for test of close
fit = .26), and a GFI = .89. However, the difference in χ² values
between the two models was not significant (Δχ² = .10, df = 2,
p > .05), providing support for the more parsimonious model
(see Table 14). Again, pathways from neighborhood structure

to perceived neighborhood (β = -1.33, std.error = .34, t = - 3.89), and from parenting style to social development (β = .55, std.error = .12, t = 4.55) were significant, as well as a positive effect of maternal education on cognitive development (β = .01, std. error = .005, t = 2.70). Fig.12 presents the standardized coefficients for each pathway.

Examination of the squared multiple correlations for the estimated variables indicated 18.42 % of the variance in sense of community, 82.08 % of the variance in satisfaction with neighborhood, and 52.87 % of the variance in perceived crime are accounted for by the latent construct of perceived neighborhood. Similarly, the latent construct of cognitive development accounted for 39.70 % of the variance in abstract reasoning, 43.13 % of the variance in quantitative reasoning, 40.94 % of the variance in short-term memory, and 44.60 % of the variance in verbal reasoning. Finally, the latent construct of social development accounted for 45.72 % of the variance in child expressiveness, 60.76 % of the variance in child warmth, and of 62.48 % of the variance in child interactiveness. Overall, the neighborhood and parenting factors together predicted 11.41 % and 24.53 % of the variance in cognitive and social development respectively.

Table 14. Fit Indices for Nested Sequence of Cross-sectional Models

Model	χ^2	df	GFI	NNF I	χ^2 diff.	df diff.
Direct effects only	288.55	84	.82	.71		
Final saturated	287.00	158	.86	.89		
Final saturated	193.14	125	.89	.93		
Reduced 1	190.20	127	.89	.93	.06	2
Reduced 2	193.30	129	.89	.94	.10	2

$^*p<.05$

CHAPTER 5

Discussion

PERCEIVED NEIGHBORHOOD SCALE

A contribution of the current study is the development of a measure of neighborhood perceptions, a self-report scale that assesses four dimensions of neighborhood life that are relevant to parents of small children. The results of the CFA performed on the PNS at two points in time indicated that the four-factor structure hypothesized is a plausible model for the observed data. Although these results are encouraging, cross validation of the factor structure of the scale in a new sample is obviously needed.

Examination of the intercorrelations among scale factors indicated significant positive correlations between social embeddedness and sense of community, and between sense of community and satisfaction with neighborhood. The significant positive associations between social embeddedness and sense of community are not surprising in light of previous operationalizations of the sense of community construct, and suggest that social interaction might be one dimension of it. For example, Glynn's (1981) definition of sense of community includes a social interaction component. Similarly, findings from two other studies reflect this association. Riger and Lavrakas (1981) found two empirically distinct but correlated factors of sense of community, one of which was social bonding (i.e., ability to identify neighbors and feeling part of the neighborhood). Weenig, Schmidt, and Midden (1990) found sense of community positively related to neighborhood cohesion.

Consistent with previous work on correlates of fear of crime (Perkins et al., 1992; Skogan, 1990) the perceived crime factor had significant loadings of items indicating both threat of crime as well as signs of incivilities. This provides indirect support for the association between physical and social incivilities and perceptions of community disorder (Lewis & Maxfield, 1980).

As expected from the available literature (Bursik & Grasmick, 1993), significant negative associations were found between perceived crime and sense of community, and between perceived crime and satisfaction with neighborhood. The latter may be explained by the fact that elevated perceptions of crime may cut off social interaction of the type needed to develop and maintain supportive networks. Further, perceived crime problems may inhibit feelings of emotional investment in the neighborhood (Taylor et al., 1985) and therefore, prevent the development of a positive sense of community sentiment.

Based on the findings of Coulton et al. (1996), greater consistency between perceived and actual ratings of neighborhood context was expected for the perceived crime and the satisfaction with neighborhood scales than for the social embeddedness and sense of community scales. The latter is probably reflected in the findings that the associations between neighborhood poverty and perceptions of crime, neighborhood poverty and satisfaction with neighborhood, and mobility and satisfaction with neighborhood were consistent over time. In contrast, the correlations between neighborhood mobility and perception of social embeddedness at the individual level were in the expected negative direction (Sampson & Groves, 1989), but not significant for either wave of data. Also, the associations between sense of community and neighborhood mobility were not consistent from Time 3 to Time 5.

Overall, these patterns of relationships may reflect differences in the extent to which the dimensions of neighborhood poverty and mobility are associated with more concrete, external referents (i.e., such as physical characteristics of the neighborhood), whereas the social and community dimensions may have more meaning at the family and individual level reflecting embeddedness in different networks of social exchange.

The pattern of correlations found among PNS scale factors and other psychological dimensions indicates that most are in the expected direction, providing evidence for construct validity. Additional evidence for the validity of the scale was obtained from the observation that findings are consistent with those reported by Taylor (1995) regarding positive associations between mothers' desire to move out of the neighborhood and perception of crime at two points in time, and between perception of crime and neighborhood deterioration at two points in time. The latter provides support for the contention that signs of disorder (e.g., physical deterioration of neighborhood) may heighten the perception of the neighborhood as a dangerous place (Lewis & Maxfield, 1980; White et al., 1987).

Consistent with findings from previous studies (Brodsky, 1996; Taylor et al., 1985) perception of crime was not associated with less participation in neighborhood activities at either point in time. As Taylor (1995) explains, actual and perceived measures of crime do not necessarily reduce social involvement in the neighborhood, and in some cases may actually drive some residents to invest more in their neighborhood organizations. Since having children appears to facilitate the development of local ties, parents may continue to invest and participate in neighborhood activities if they perceive that involvement will benefit their children.

NEIGHBORHOOD INFLUENCES ON DEVELOPMENT

Findings from both the longitudinal and cross-sectional models fitted suggest no direct effects of neighborhood structure—

at least, as captured by the demographic indices considered—
on children's development. The absence of relationships
between neighborhood structure and child development may
be due to several factors. First, the relationship between contextual factors and child development may be small in magnitude (Elliot, Wilson, Huizinga, Sampson, Elliot & Rankin,
1996). Second, insufficient power due to small sample size, as
well as, lack of sufficient variability within the sample may
have prevented observing the expected effects.

Another possible explanation is that the indicators of neighborhood structure included in the models tested are still very
distal from the processes that ultimately relate to child development. Effects of neighborhood context might be indirectly
operating through processes at the neighborhood and/or family
level not specified in the models tested. As Tienda (1991) suggests, global characteristics of the ecological area—such as
existing formal and informal institutions—may be more proximal determinants of interaction patterns among residents, and
ultimately influence child outcomes. Although neighborhood
demographics have been linked with individual-level variables
(Brooks-Gunn et al., 1993) available data for this study were not
suitable to address the neighborhood-level phenomena.
Because families in the sample were scattered across 66 census
tracts, the number of observations by census tract was not large
enough to aggregate data at the neighborhood level.

If, indeed, the neighborhood structure measure is assessing distal factors and treating them as independent variables,
then it might not be an adequate measure of context. That is,
indicators might fail to capture other relevant features of the
neighborhood such as informal, formal, and institutional
structures available for the interactions between families, and
their links with the opportunity structure.

A related issue has to do with the emphasis that the census indicators of neighborhood structure place on disadvantage. That is, they might fail to capture positive characteristics of the neighborhood such as assets and resources. The latter is supported by the observation that the pattern of signifi-

cant loadings for the neighborhood structure factor was reflecting, to a large extent, poverty and marginality (i.e., welfare dependence, male unemployment, female-headed families). The focus on neighborhood disadvantage may overlook important resource differences among neighborhood tracts that may be ultimately related to outcome. Further, because the majority of sample participants resided in inner-city tracts, a measure of neighborhood centered on disadvantage is likely to exhibit low variability within the sample.

The observation that census indicators of mobility had a weak loading on the neighborhood structure construct, and no significant associations with child development is consistent with findings from Korbin and Coulton (1997). In their study, instability (i.e., degree to which the area could be characterized by movement of residents) had the weakest effect on maltreatment rates. The latter may suggest that is not the movement of residents per se that might affect the ecology of neighborhoods, but rather the composition of mobility. It is apparent that residential mobility may have different consequences on neighborhood social organization depending on whether it represents an increase in homeowners or an increase in renters or transient residents. Similarly, the meaning of mobility for neighborhood life might be different in affluent as opposed to impoverished areas (Campbell & Lee, 1992).

The finding that indicators of neighborhood poverty were not significantly related to child development is not consistent with the strong associations between neighborhood poverty and child maltreatment reported by previous studies (Coulton et al., 1995; Deccio et al., 1994; Korbin and Coulton,1997). Possible explanations for the differences are the different domains (i.e., focused on social problems as opposed to normative development) and the different level of analysis of the outcome measures—aggregate level (Korbin & Coulton, 1997) as opposed to individual level in the current study. Additionally, the census tracts sampled in the Coulton et al. study included a wider range of socioeconomic levels. A restriction of range due to homogeneity in poverty levels might have decreased the magnitude of the correlations in the current sample.

Support for the assumption that stronger linkages with child development would be found by incorporating a measure of perceived neighborhood was found in its significant longitudinal association with social development. However, the direction (i.e., negative) of this association is hard to interpret. Overall, findings suggest that negative perceptions of the neighborhood (i.e., low social embeddedness, low sense of community, low neighborhood satisfaction, and high perceptions of crime) are associated with better social development. One possible explanation for this finding is that maternal perceptions of lack of resources and threats in the neighborhood may increase parental involvement in the development of children. Findings from qualitative studies (Furstenberg, 1993; Korbin & Coulton, 1997) indicate that parental vigilance is enhanced in dangerous neighborhoods, with parents reporting the need to do more parenting and supervision of their children. In a similar way, perceptions of crime and/or lack of resources in the neighborhood could translate into more opportunities for activities and interaction with parents because of the restricted opportunities for children to play outside on their own.

Another explanation is that negative assessments of the neighborhood may drive parents to look for opportunities (i.e., day care, preschool programs) outside their neighborhood (Burton & Jarrett, 1991) that might benefit their children's development. Previous studies (Furstenberg, 1993; Jarrett, 1995) describe that searching for opportunities and accessing resources outside the neighborhood of residence—either through kinship or organizational networks—are important community-bridging strategies of families who find a way out of poverty (i.e., successful families living in high-risk environments). Still, other variables at the family level may be intervening to account for this association.

Another possibility is to conceive that it is not the neighborhood per se that makes a difference on development but the fit between neighborhood resources and parental engagement in opportunities (Coleman, 1988). To test this kind of premise would require the collection of information on both the availability of neighborhood resources (i.e., organizations, programs, groups, and settings) and actual involvement of families in them.

The above view is consistent with the transactional perspective that views families and neighborhoods as interdependent systems reciprocally influencing one another to produce developmental outcomes. In this line, perceptions of neighborhood opportunities may be important for child development when parents are capturing available resources that can be mobilized for the well-being of children. Alternatively, perceptions of threat and disadvantage may warn parents that particular management strategies are needed in order for children to survive and thrive.

Findings from previous studies support the assumption that parents, to the extent possible, locate and select desirable environments for their families, channeling their children's access to favorable settings within the neighborhood, or at least segregating them from undesirable ones (Furstenberg, 1993). For example, Burton (1991) documents how families living in neighborhoods driven by a drug-dealing economy accommodate their child care arrangements and strategies to protect their children. In brief, examination of the fit between perceptions of neighborhood threats and parental responsiveness to cope with these threats may clarify the nature of the association between neighborhood perceptions and social development.

According to the collective socialization hypothesis (Jencks & Meyer, 1990), the strength and salience of bonds and the sense of reciprocal obligations of the family can mediate the influences of neighborhood structure on child development. Although no tests of this hypothesis were performed in this study, cross-sectional findings suggest that the sense of community component (i.e., sense of belongingness, sense of mutual influence, shared emotional connection) rather than social embeddedness (i.e., frequency of social exchanges with

neighbors) had the strongest association with social development. Because the association was negative, findings are in
line with those reported by Brodsky (1996) in the sense that
not feeling part of the community can have positive effects for
families living in high-risk environments. Further, this finding points to the dynamic role that parental perceptions (i.e.,
identification of threats and resources both within or outside
the neighborhood) may play in guiding parents' social
exchanges and involvement in the community.

The pathways through which maternal perceptions might
influence social development remain unknown. Although the
current findings stress the effects of proximal factors such as
family factors (i.e., maternal perceptions and parenting) on
social development, the hypothesized mediational effect of
parenting could not be tested in this study.

Alternatively, the association between perceived neighborhood and social development could be accounted for by
other variables. For example, at the level of family processes,
the possibility that the longitudinal perceived neighborhood
effects on social development may be accounted for by day-to-
day family interaction processes can not be ruled out from the
models tested. During the two-year period of the study, daily
exchanges between parents and children have taken place that
are not controlled for in the models fitted. Further, it is possible to think that not only family processes are mutually
influencing with children's social behavior, but that family
and neighborhood processes are influencing each other as
well. The nature of these influences could be best captured
through autoregressive models.

The finding that parental warmth is positively associated
with social development is certainly consistent with the findings of a long tradition of research on the effects of parental
practices (Baumrind, 1971, 1996; Cohn et al., 1992; Pratt et al.,
1988) on children's development. During the preschool years,
family efforts at socialization are very strong and children
might spend little time in the neighborhood without family
supervision. At later stages, when family control diminishes

and children have more opportunities to spend time in unsupervised activities in the neighborhood, the effects of neighborhoods might be more visible. Thus, it is likely that the young children studied had only limited direct exposure to neighborhood factors.

STRENGTHS OF THE STUDY

Three advantages of the current study are its focus on preschool children (i.e., a population that has not been researched enough), the use of multiple sources of data (i.e., self-report, observational, standardized developmental assessments, census ratings), and the modeling of longitudinal effects of neighborhood characteristics on child development.

Few studies have explored mechanisms of neighborhood effects (Gephart, 1989). The current study moved one step forward in trying to understand the ways in which neighborhoods relate to children's development, and the relationships among neighborhood structure, family processes, and children's outcomes.

Departing from previous quantitative research that had examined the effects of socioeconomic composition and racial mix of neighborhoods on individual outcomes (Crane, 1991; Jencks & Meyer, 1990) the current study added the dimension of social interaction to the study of neighborhood effects. Social interaction is one mechanism through which neighborhoods are thought to affect individuals (Gephart, 1989). Current findings supported the association between neighborhood social exchanges and social development of children, though not in the expected direction.

Previous studies have seldom distinguished the effects of neighborhoods from the effects of neighbors. Both dimensions were captured in the current study using different sources of data, and findings suggest that only the latter are related to social development. Through the models tested, the study linked micro (i.e., maternal perceptions, parent-child interactions) and macrolevel (i.e., census demographic ratings) dimensions of social behavior.

LIMITATIONS OF THE STUDY

Was the neighborhood unit defined relevant to the domain of interest? A difficult issue is how to characterize neighborhoods in ways that best link their properties (i.e., social and personal variation) to the outcome of interest (Gephart, 1989), in this case, child development. In interpreting the current findings, it can not be assumed that structural ratings of census tracts in fact reflect neighborhood. They are imperfect proxies for neighborhood for several reasons. First, the use of census sociodemographic ratings to describe neighborhood environments corresponds to what Bronfenbrenner (1986) has called the "social address" paradigm. Within this paradigm, individuals are typically ascribed certain contextual experiences—the environmental label—based on the social address of their current geographic residence. This view gives no consideration to the intervening structures or processes through which the environment might relate to the course of development (Bronfenbrenner & Crouter, 1983).

Second, as Burton et al. (1997) suggest, using the children's current geographic residences as the "locators" of contextual experiences may be particularly misleading when studying the development of ethnic minority children. For example, research on African American families suggests that family arrangements are flexible and fluid. Because families live coresidentially and extra-residentially (Gordon, Chase-Lansdale, Matjasko, & Brooks-Gunn, 1997; Martin & Martin, 1978; Stack, 1974; Taylor, 1986), both within and across neighborhoods, children may experience a multiplicity of neighborhoods of residence. Therefore, using one residential address as the identifier of the primary neighborhood for a child may not provide an accurate view of the impact of neighborhood on developmental outcomes because the effects of multiple neighborhoods of residence are not captured. The fluency of coresidence patterns observed in African American families can be confounded with the issue of residential mobility described for families living in poverty. In order to differentiate family (i.e., availability of caregivers, family support) and neighborhood effects on development it is important to map trajectories of family moves (i.e., to the same or different neighborhoods) and patterns of coresidence.

Alternatively, having information on the multiple neighborhoods that children might experience will certainly provide evidence for exposure to the social environments that allegedly influence their behavior. This is important in the light of the evidence that chronically poor people change their residence frequently.

Third, census indicators are static in that they assume no temporal variation (i.e., daily, seasonal) of the neighborhood environments. However, neighborhoods have daily and seasonal variations in rhythms, interaction patterns, and routines (Burton et al., 1997; Werner, 1987) that need to be considered to obtain valid measurements of the neighborhood characteristics that allegedly influence development. Differences in rhythms and behavioral patterns should be taken into consideration before attributing developmental outcomes to neighborhood effects.

Fourth, census socioeconomic composition measures may not provide information on the quality of neighborhood processes and contexts that can be obtained from direct observation of the physical environment, neighborhood interaction, and assessment of resources (Burton et al., 1997). Census tracts essentially represent "statistical" neighborhoods (Tienda, 1991) and may not correspond with the neighborhood of interaction or of self-location by residents. Moreover, insofar as neighborhood has a geographical referent, its meaning depends upon context and function. Because neighborhood-level processes may define the context for associational networks and family interaction, and therefore relate to children's development, they may be more likely to mediate the effects of neighborhood structure. For example, census tract data may not differentiate between housing projects and single family homes.

As Walker and Furstenberg (1994) suggest, several social processes may mediate the effects of local neighborhood context: (a) within neighborhoods social processes of inclusion and exclusion (e.g., by social class or racial stratification) may be related to parenting strategies; (b) parents' cultural expectations may be related to involvement and participation in their communities; and (c) individual networks that extend beyond neighborhoods seem equally important in determining the resources that parents have (e.g., availability of social support, access to opportunities).

The processes outlined above suggest that it might not be the neighborhood per se that makes a difference for child development but the fit between neighborhood resources and parental engagement in opportunities (Coleman, 1988).

The latter view is consistent with the transactional perspective (Lynch & Cicchetti, 1998) that views children and neighborhoods as interdependent systems reciprocally influencing one another to produce developmental outcomes. Although for the age period examined in this study interactions between children and neighborhoods may be invariably mediated by family (Burton et al., 1997) it seems equally important to consider the effects that children may have on their neighborhood environments particularly at older ages. Unfortunately, the available data does not allow this transactional type of analysis.

The relevant unit to define neighborhoods depends upon the outcome or process of interest. Because the focus of the study is on the development of small children other features of the neighborhood such as the availability of day care facilities, programs targeting young children, number and quality of schools, availability of health care providers, libraries, and playgrounds may be important indicators of the quality of the neighborhood environment.

Differences observed in the associations between neighborhood constructs (i.e., structure and perceived) and children's development possibly reflect the fact that the two measures do not correspond to the same neighborhood. Findings from the cross-sectional models indicated a significant negative relationship between the two measures. Because census tracts do not necessarily represent the neighborhood as it would be defined by residents and they may be more heterogeneous than would be true of the residents' perceived neighborhood (Korbin & Coulton, 1997), their associations with children's development are expected to be different.

The ecological validity of the parenting style measure is questionable in the sense that it may not capture the strategies that parents use to manage their children's behavior in the neighborhood context. Parenting scales were derived from a laboratory setting observation of mother-child interaction that may not reproduce the interaction that takes place in the neighborhood context (i.e., lacks the threats and challenges of the real world). Standardized laboratory observations could overlook relevant aspects of the parenting behavior as they occur in context. For example, the measure might not capture the parenting strategies used to manage the external environment. In brief, the measure may lack contextual validity to examine the parenting processes hypothesized to mediate perceived neighborhood influences.

The times of measurement may not have been the best to capture the effects hypothesized. As mentioned earlier, very few studies have examined neighborhood effects in small children. The possibility that effects of neighborhood structure may be visible when children are older can not be ruled out. Findings from adolescent studies suggest that neighborhood effects are minimal on young children and stronger on older youths who become increasingly embedded in neighborhood social networks and have longer periods of exposure to the risks of disorganized neighborhoods (Kasarda & Janowitz, 1974; McLeod & Shanahan, 1994). A similar trend could be expected for younger children. That is, depending on duration and time of exposure, neighborhood effects may well be more visible when children are older and spend more time in the neighborhood.

Parental strategies to deal with neighborhood disadvantage may be selectively activated when children are older. Because the family processes that high-risk environments—such as inner-city neighborhoods—bring about represent ways to manage the external environment (i.e., world outside the home), there might be fewer opportunities for parents to display these strategies because their preschool children are not spending a considerable amount of time in the neighborhood.

Alternatively, parental strategies may be selectively activated by child gender, but more likely among adolescents. Because gender effects seem unlikely in preschoolers, and in consideration of the small sample size no gender differences were examined in the present study. The small sample size also precluded controlling for the association that other family characteristics such as type of household (e.g., single versus multiple caregivers) might have with child development. For example, the availability of caregivers has been positively associated with social development (Gordon et al. 1997) and lower rates of child maltreatment (Coulton et al., 1996).

Finally, an important methodological limitation refers to the stability of the models fitted. Because the statistical properties of full-information estimation methods depend on large-samples a natural concern with the current findings is the meaningfulness of parameter estimates. Results from the current models might be unstable due to small sample size. Therefore, the models tested remain to be fully validated.

DIRECTIONS FOR FUTURE RESEARCH

As Tienda (1991) stated, determining neighborhood effects on individual behavior poses formidable conceptual and methodological challenges. The neighborhood as a context encompasses dimensions at different levels of analysis—individual, family, and community—that need to be taken into consideration at each stage of the research design.

Though evidence is still inconclusive regarding the pathways through which neighborhood perceptions are associated with child social development, current findings highlight the need to further specify and test intervening mechanisms at the family level (Gephart, 1989).

Because of the dynamic nature of neighborhood, family, and individual development, understanding the nature of the effects of neighborhoods on individuals calls for longitudinal studies. Demonstrating neighborhood influences requires identifying the processes in the immediate milieu that affect the cumulative experiences of children as they develop over time. In other words, there is a need to attend to the life course longitudinally, not simply to outcomes or status at a single point in time. In addition, developmental stage issues may be critical in relation to children's age of exposure to events and conditions "on the street" in inner-city neighborhoods.

Because existing sources of data may be not well suited to address the questions posed (e.g., mechanisms linking neighborhood and family variables) collection of new data will be necessary (Furstenberg & Hughes, 1997). Multilevel data sets—those which include characteristics of neighborhoods, schools, families, and individuals—will be needed. Further, an approach combining quantitative and qualitative methods of data collection and analyses may be the best strategy for future research. For example, certain characteristics such as social organization and institutional functioning of neighborhoods require community study or ethnographic observation and are likely to yield more powerful linkages with phenomena at the family level.

Ideally, collecting data on processes at different levels (i.e., child, family, neighborhood) and from different sources may be most suitable to clarifying the nature of direct and indirect effects of neighborhoods on child development.

IMPLICATIONS FOR INTERVENTION

An important reason for the growing interest on the impact that neighborhood contexts have on children and their families is the potential for preventive intervention that these contexts entail. Overall, findings from the current study suggest that the geographical (i.e., site or place) neighborhood should not be the only target for intervention when trying to foster children's development. Findings also suggest that interventions addressed to African American inner-city families should go beyond ameliorating levels of neighborhood poverty.

Current findings highlight the active role of the family in dealing with the disadvantages and threats of high-risk neighborhoods in preschool children. The observation that perceptions of neighborhood matter for social development suggests that intervention could be targeted at the family level particularly when families perceive disadvantages in their neighborhoods. However, pathways through which maternal perceptions influence social development remain unknown and therefore, cannot yet inform the design of intervention programs.

Strategies designed to promote better development of children should probably focus on both strengthening at-risk families (i.e., enhancing family resources) and improving the quality of life in at-risk neighborhoods (i.e., enhancing community resources).

APPENDIX 1

Structural Equation Modeling

The model-building task in SEM can be thought of as the analysis of two conceptually distinct models: (a) the measurement model, and (b) the structural model (Anderson & Gerbing, 1988). The measurement model prescribes latent variables; that is, it specifies the relations of the observed variables to their posited underlying constructs. Latent variables are unobserved variables implied by the covariances among two or more indicators. The structural component prescribes the relations between latent variables and observed variables that are not indicators of latent variables, as posited by some theory.

Given a set of measured and latent variables, a SEM model postulates a pattern of linear relationships among these variables. Within a model, hypothesized relationships can be defined as either directional or nondirectional and each latent variable can be defined as either endogeneous or exogeneous (MacCallum, 1995). Directional relationships represent hypothesized linear directional influences of one variable on another. Nondirectional relationships represent hypothesized correlational associations between variables, with no attempt to postulate direction of influence. Numerical values associated with directional relationships are values of regression coefficients; that is, weights applied to variables in linear regression equations. Numerical values associated with nondirectional relationships are values of covariances between variables (or correlations, if variables are standardized). These weights and covariances can be thought of as parameters of the model.

Latent variables can be designated as either endogenous or exogenous. An endogenous variable is one that receives a directional influence from some other variable in the system. An exogenous variable is one that does not receive a directional influence from any other variable in the system (MacCallum, 1995). An endogenous latent variable will generally be specified as being influenced also by an error term—the disturbance term—representing that part of the latent variable not accounted for by the linear influences of the other variables specified in the model (MacCallum, 1995). Thus, disturbance terms consist partly of random error and partly of systematic error that is not explained, but could theoretically be explained by variables or effects not included in the model.

Types of fit indexes

Evaluation of the fit of a SEM can refer to one of two characteristics of the model:

1. Absolute fit concerns the degree to which the covariances implied by the fixed and free parameters specified in the model match the observed covariances from which free parameters in the model are estimated. Indexes of absolute fit typically gauge lack of fit; that is, optimal fit is indicated by a value of zero, and increasing values indicate greater departure of the implied covariance matrix from the observed covariance matrix.

2. Incremental fit concerns the degree to which the model in question is superior to an alternative model, usually one that specifies no covariances among variables (i.e., the "null" or independence model) in reproducing the observed covariances. Indexes of incremental fit typically gauge "goodness of fit"; that is, larger values indicate greater improvement of the model in question over an alternative model in reproducing the observed covariances.

A further distinction between absolute and incremental fit indexes can be made (Bollen, 1989). An absolute fit index directly assesses how well an a priori model reproduces the sample data. These indexes make an implicit or an explicit comparison to a saturated model that exactly reproduces the observed covariance matrix. In contrast, incremental or comparative fit indexes measure the proportionate improvement in fit by comparing a target model with a more restricted, nested baseline model. A null model in which all the observed variables are uncorrelated is the most typically used baseline model. For further distinctions between incremental fit indexes see Hu and Bentler (1995).

A critical issue to keep in mind in model specification and evaluation is the degree of disconfirmability of the model. For a model to be disconfirmable to any degree, the effective number of parameters must be less than the number of measured variables' variances/covariances; that is, the model will have positive degrees of freedom. Therefore, in the assessment of model fit it is essential to take into account the degree of disconfirmability of a model (Hoyle, 1995). The latter can be examined by considering the root mean square error of approximation (RMSEA), which is essentially a measure of lack of fit per degree of freedom. The RMSEA index takes the parsimony of the model into account (i.e., the number of parameters fixed versus the number of parameters free to be estimated), and it is a direct measure of the discrepancy between the estimated covariation matrix and the matrix implied by the specified model.

Finally, the Cross-Validation Index (CVI) provides an indication of how well a solution obtained from a sample of a given size would fit in an independently drawn sample.

Pearson Correlations Coefficients for Variables in Longitudinal Models

	1	2	3	4	5	6	7	8	9	10	11	12
1. Maternal educa.												
2. Poverty	-.29***											
3. Unemployment	-.25**	.79***										
4. Rental housing	-.27**	.85***	.60***									
5. S.Embeddedness	-.05	.10	.10	.06								
6. S.Community	.10	-.13	-.13	-.15	.63***							
7. Satisfaction	.13	-.31***	-.31***	-.32***	.30***	.57***						
8. Perceived Crime	-.13	.30***	.27**	.27**	-.07	-.38***	.63***					
9. Parent warmth	.01	.08	.08	.03	-.01	-.04	.15	-.04				
10. Parent structure	.02	-.04	-.05	-.06	-.01	-.05	.11	-.08	.65***			
11. Quantitative reas.	.17	.00	-.13	-.06	-.02	-.10	.04	-.05	.23**	.26**		
12. Verbal reas.	.33***	-.13	-.17	-.21**	-.06	-.07	.12	-.11	.15	.25**	.43***	
13. Short term mem.	.22**	-.19*	-.14	-.11	.06	.04	.24**	-.08	-.03	.14	.29***	.51***
14. Abstract reas.	.18*	-.14	-.11	-.11	-.17	-.09	.16	-.15	.14	.18*	.46***	.43***
15. Child warmth	.19*	-.08	-.05	-.17*	-.29**	-.25**	-.00	.05	.06	.06	.27**	.24**
16. Child task	.06	-.03	.01	-.01	-.00	-.01	.02	-.01	-.00	.06	.13	.08

* $p<.05$; ** $p<.01$; *** $p<.001$

Pearson Correlation Coefficients for Variables in Cross-sectional Models

	1	2	3	4	5	6	7	8	9	10	11	12
1. Maternal educa.												
2. Poverty	-.21**											
3. Unemployment	-.18**	.80***										
4. Rental housing	-.19**	.89***	.66***									
5. S.Embeddedness	.03	.01	.05	-.00								
6. S.Community	.17**	-.24***	-.14*	-.22**	.54***							
7. Satisfaction	.20**	-.46***	-.38***	-.37***	.09	.39***						
8. Perceived Crime	-.13	.40***	.34***	.28***	.01	-.28***	.69***					
9. Parent warmth	.02	-.10	.01	-.09	.01	.13	.13	-.05				
10. Parent structure	.06	-.14*	-.14*	-.05	.18**	.12	.13	-.08	.38***			
11. Quantitative reas.	.12	-.01	-.08	-.01	-.03	.00	.05	-.09	-.09**	.01		
12. Verbal reas.	.22**	-.17**	-.20**	-.22**	-.09	.05	.14*	-.14*	.05	.09	.49***	
13. Short term mem.	.11	-.07	-.05	-.07	-.06	.17*	.14	-.12	-.04	.10	.41***	.55***
14. Abstract reas.	.17**	-.09	-.07	-.05	-.05	.07	.14*	-.16*	-.02	.03	.54***	.39***
15. Child warmth	.05	-.01	.05	-.04	-.02	-.08	.03	-.00	.21**	.09	.11	.19*
16. Child task	.02	.02	.07	.04	-.00	.01	-.07	.04	.10	.30***	-.09	.13

* $p<.05$; ** $p<.01$; *** $p<.001$

References

Anderson, E. (1991). Neighborhood effects on teenage pregnancy. In J. C. Jencks & P. Peterson (Eds.), *The urban underclass* (pp. 375–398). Washington, DC: The Brookings Institution.

Anderson, J., & Gerbing, D. (1988). Structural equation modeling in practice: A review and recommended two-step approach. *Psychological Bulletin*, 103(3), 411–423.

Argyle, M., & Henderson, M. (1985). *The anatomy of relationships.* London: Heineman.

Bane, M. & Ellwood, D. (1986, Winter). Slipping into and out of poverty: The dynamics of spells. *Journal of Human Resources*, 21, 1–23.

Barry, F. (1994). A neighborhood based approach: What is it? In G. Melton & F. Barry (Eds.), *Protecting children from abuse and neglect* (pp.14–39). New York: The Guilford Press.

Baron, R. & Kenny, D. (1986). The moderator-mediator distinction in social psychological research: Conceptual, strategic, and statistical considerations. *Journal of Personality and Social Psychology*, 51(6), 1173–1182.

Baumrind, D. (1971). Current theories of parental authority. *Developmental Psychology Monograph*, 4(1), part 2.

Baumrind, D. (1994). The social context of child maltreatment. *Family Relations*, 43, 360–368.

Baumrind, D. (1996). Parenting: The discipline controversy revisited. *Family Relations*, 45, 405–414.

Bell, C., & Jenkins, E. (1993). Community violence and children on Chicago's southside. *Psychiatry*, 56, 46–53.

Belle, D. (1982). *Lives in stress*. Newbury Park, CA: Sage.

Belle, D. (1983). The impact of poverty on social networks and support. In L. Lein & M. Sussman (Eds.), *The ties that bind: Men's and women's social networks*. New York: Haworth.

Bentler, P. & Bonett, D. (1980). Significance tests and goodness-of-fit in the analysis of covariance structures. *Psychological Bulletin, 88*, 588–606.

Berry, B., & Kasarda, J. (1977). *Contemporary urban ecology*. New York: Macmillan.

Black, M., Dubowitz, H., & Starr, R. (in press). African American fathers in low-income, urban families: Development, behavior, and home environment of their 3-year old children. *Child Development*.

Bollen, K. (1989). A new incremental fit index for general structural equation models. *Sociological Methods and Research, 17*, 303–316.

Brewster, K. (1994). Neighborhood context and the transition to sexual activity among young, black women. *Demography, 31*(4), 603–614.

Brodsky, A. (1996). Resilient single mothers in risky neighborhoods: Negative psychological sense of community. *Journal of Community Psychology, 24*(4), 347–363.

Bronfenbrenner, U. (1979). *The ecology of human development*. Cambridge, MA: Harvard University Press.

Bronfenbrenner, U. (1986). Ecology of family as a context for human development. *Developmental Psychology, 22*(6), 732–742.

Bronfenbrenner, U., & Crouter, A. (1983). The evolution of environmental models in developmental research. In W. Kessen (Ed.), *History, theory, and methods*. Vol. 1 of P. H. Mussen (Ed.), *Handbook of child psychology* (4th ed.). New York: Wiley.

Brooks-Gunn, J. (1990). Identifying the vulnerable young child. In D. Rogers & E. Ginzberg, (Eds.), *Improving the life chances of children at risk*, (pp. 104–124). Boulder, CO: Westview Press.

Brooks-Gunn, J. (1996). Children in families in communities: Risk and intervention in the Bronfenbrenner tradition. In P. Moen, G. Elder, & K. Luscher (Eds.), *Examining lives in con-*

text (pp. 467–519). Washington, DC: American Psychological Association.

Brooks-Gunn, J., Duncan, G., Klebanov, P., & Sealand, N. (1993). Do neighborhoods influence child and adolescent development? *American Journal of Sociology, 99*(2), 353–395.

Brooks-Gunn, J., & Furstenberg, F. (1986). The children of adolescent mothers: Physical, academic and psychological outcomes. *Developmental Review, 6,* 224–251.

Brooks-Gunn, J.,& Furstenberg, F. (1987). Continuity and change in the context of poverty: Adolescent mothers and their children. In J. Gallagher & C. Ramey (Eds.), *The malleability of children* (pp. 171–187). Baltimore, MD: Brookes.

Brooks-Gunn, J., Guo, G., & Furstenberg, F. (1993). Who drops out and who continues beyond high school? A 20-year follow-up of black urban youth. *Journal of Research on Adolescence, 3*(3), 271–294.

Browne, M., & Cudeck, R. (1993). Alternative ways of assessing model fit. In K. Bollen & J. Long (Eds.), *Testing structural equation models* (pp. 136– 162). Newbury Park, CA: Sage.

Bryant, B. (1985). The neighborhood walk: Sources of support in middle childhood. *Monographs of the Society for Research in Child Development, 50*(3, serial No. 210).

Bulmer, M. (1986). *Neighbors: The work of Phillip Abram.* Cambridge, England: Cambridge University Press.

Bursik, R. (1986). Delinquency rates as sources of ecological change. In J. Byrne & R. Sampson (Eds.), *The social ecology of crime* (pp. 63–74). New York: Springer-Verlag.

Bursik, R. (1988). Social disorganization and theories of crime and delinquency: Problems and prospects. *Criminology, 26,* 519–551.

Bursik, R. J., & Grasmick, H. (1993). *Neighborhoods and crime.* New York: Lexington Books.

Burton, L. (1991). Caring for children in high-risk neighborhoods. *The American Enterprise,* May/June, 34–37.

Burton, L., & Jarrett, R. (1991, August). *Studying African American family structure and process in underclass neighborhoods: Conceptual considerations.* Paper presented at the annual meeting of the American Sociological Association, Cincinnati, Ohio.

Burton, L., Price-Spratlen, T., & Spencer, M. (1997). On ways of thinking about measuring neighborhoods: Implications for studying context and development among minority children. In J. Brooks-Gunn, G. Duncan, & L. Aber (Eds.), *Neighborhood poverty: Context and consequences for children* (pp. 132– 144). New York: Russell Sage.

Campbell, K., & Lee, B. (1992). Gender differences in urban neigh boring. *Sociological Quarterly, 31*, 495–512.

Campbell, K., & Lee, B. (1992). Sources of personal neighbor net works: Social integration, need or time? *Social Forces, 70*(4), 1077–1100.

Campbell, F., & Ramey, C. (1994). Effects of early intervention on intellectual and academic achievement: A follow-up study of children from low-income families. *Child Development, 65*, 684–698.

Chase-Lansdale, P. L. & Brooks-Gunn, J. (Eds.) (1995). *Escape from poverty*. New York: Cambridge University Press.

Chase-Lansdale, P. L., Brooks-Gunn, J., & Zamsky, E. (1994). Young African American multigenerational families in poverty: Quality of mothering and grandmothering. *Child Development, 65*, 373–393.

Chavis, D., Hogge, J., McMillan, D., & Wandersman, A. (1986). Sense of community through Brunswik's lens: A first look. *Journal of Community Psychology, 14*, 24–40.

Chavis, D., & Wandersman, A. (1990). Sense of community in the urban environment: A catalyst for participation and community development. *American Journal of Community Psychology, 18*, 55–81.

Chou, C. & Bentler, P. (1995). Estimates and tests in structural equation modeling. In Hoyle, R. (Ed.), *Structural equation modeling* (pp. 37–55). Thousand Oaks, CA: Sage.

Cicchetti, D., & Lynch, M. (1993). Toward an ecological/transactional model of community violence and child maltreatment: Consequences for children's development. *Psychiatry, 56*, 96–118.

Clemente, F., & Kleiman, F. (1977). Fear of crime in the U.S.: A multivariate analysis. *Social Forces, 56,* 519–531.

Cochran, M. (1988). Parental empowerment in family matters: Lessons learned from a research program. In D. Powell (Ed.), *Parent education and support programs: Consequences for children and family* (pp. 33–34). New York: Ablex.

Cochran, M. & Brassard, J. (1979). Child development and personal social networks. *Child Development, 50,* 601–615.

Cochran, M., Larner, M., Riley, D., Gunnarsson, L., & Henderson, C. (1990). *Extending families: The social networks of parents and the children.* Cambridge, England: The Cambridge University Press.

Cohen, S., & Wills, T. (1985). Stress, social support, and the buffering hypothesis. *Psychological Bulletin, 98,* 310–357.

Cohn, D., Cowan, P., Cowan, C., & Pearson, J. (1992). Mothers' and fathers' working models of childhood attachment relationships, parenting styles, and child behavior. *Development and Psychopathology, 4,* 417–431.

Coleman, J. (1988). Social capital in the creation of human capital. *American Journal of Sociology, 94,* 95–120.

Comrey, A. & Lee, H. (1992). *A first course in factor analysis.* NJ: Erlbaum.

Coulton, C., Korbin, J., & Su, M. (1996). Measuring neighborhood context for young children in an urban area. *American Journal of Community Psychology, 24*(1), 5–32.

Coulton, C., Korbin, J., Su, M. & Chow, J. (1995). Community level factors and child maltreatment rates. *Child Development, 66,* 1262–1276.

Coulton, C., & Pandey, S. (1992). Geographic concentration of poverty and risk to children in urban neighborhoods. *American Behavioral Scientist, 35*(3), 238–257.

Covington, J., & Taylor, R. (1991). Fear of crime in urban residential neighborhoods: Implications of between and within-neighborhood sources for current models. *The Sociological Quarterly, 32,* 231–249.

Crane, J. (1991). Effects of neighborhoods on dropping out of school and teenage childbearing. In J. C. Jencks & P. Peterson (Eds.),

The urban underclass (pp. 299–320). Washington, DC: The Brookings Institution.

Crimmins, E., & Ingegneri, D. (1990). Interaction and living arrangements of older parents and their children. *Research on Aging, 12*, 3–35.

Crittenden, P. (1985). Social networks, quality of child rearing, and child development. *Child Development, 56*, 1299–1313.

Crnic, K., & Greenberg, M. (1990). Minor parenting stresses with young children. *Child Development, 61*, 1628–1637.

Deccio, G., Horner, W., & Wilson, D. (1994). High-risk neighbor hoods and high-risk families: Replication research related to the human ecology of child maltreatment. *Journal of Social Service Research, 18*(3/4), 123–137.

Dodge, K., Pettit, G. & Bates, J. (1994). Socialization mediators of the relation between socioeconomic status and child conduct problems. *Child Development, 65*, 649–665.

Dornbusch, S. (1989). The sociology of adolescence. *Annual Review of Sociology, 15*, 233–259.

Drake, B., & Pandey, S. (1996). Understanding the relationship between neighborhood poverty and specific types of child maltreatment. *Child Abuse and Neglect, 20*(11), 1003–1018.

DuBow, F. & Emmons, D. (1981). The community hypothesis. In D. Lewis (Ed.), *Reactions to crime* (pp. 167–181). Newbury Park, CA: Sage.

Duncan, G., Brooks-Gunn, J., & Klebanov, P. (1994). Economic depri vation and early child development. *Child Development, 65* (1), 296–318.

Dunst, C. J., Jenkins, V., & Trivette, C. M. (1984). The family support scale: Reliability and validity. *Journal of Individual, Family, and Community Wellness, 1*, 45–52.

Edelman, M. (1987). *Families in peril: An agenda for social change.* Cambridge, MA: Harvard University Press.

Elder, G., & Caspi, A. (1988). Economic stress in lives: Developmental perspectives. *Journal of Social Issues, 44*, 25–45.

Elliot, D., Wilson, W., Huizinga, D., Sampson, R., Elliot, A. & Rankin, B. (1996). The effects of neighborhood disadvantage on child development. *Journal of Research in Crime and Delinquency, 33*(4), 389–426.

Ensminsger, M., Lamkin, R. & Jacobson, N. (1996). School leaving: A longitudinal perspective including neighborhood effects. *Child Development, 67,* 2400–2416.

Ferraro, K. (1994). *Fear of crime: Interpreting victimization risk.* Albany, NY: State University of New York Press.

Forrest, R., & Allan, M. (1991). Transformation through tenure? The early purchasers of council houses, 1968–1973. *Journal of Social Policy, 20,* 1–25.

Furstenberg, F. (1993). How families manage risk and opportunity in dangerous neigborhoods. In W. J. Wilson (Ed.), *Sociology and the public agenda* (pp. 231–258). Newbury Park, CA: Sage.

Furstenberg, F., & Hughes, M. (1997). The influence of neighborhoods on children's development: A theoretical perspective and a research agenda. In J. Brooks-Gunn, G. Duncan, & L. Aber (Eds.), *Neighborhood poverty: Context and consequences for children* (pp. 23–47). New York: Russell Sage.

Furstenberg, F., Levine, J., & Brooks-Gunn, J. (1990). The daughters of teenage mothers: Patterns of early childbearing in two generations. *Family Planning Perspectives, 22*(2), 54–61.

Gambrill, E., & Paquin, G. (1992). Neighbors: A neglected resource. *Children and Youth Services Review, 14,* 253–272.

Garbarino, J., & Crouter, A. (1978). Defining the community context for parent child relations: The correlates of child maltreatment. *Child Development, 49,* 604–616.

Garbarino, J., & Kostelny, K. (1994). Neighborhood-based programs. In G. Melton & F. Barry (Eds.), *Protecting children from abuse and neglect* (pp. 304–352). New York: The Guilford Press.

Garbarino, J., Kostelny, K., & Dubrow, N. (1991). What children can tell us about living in danger. *American Psychologist, 46*(4), 376–383.

Garbarino, J., & Sherman, D. (1980). Identifying high-risk neighbor hoods. In J. Garbarino, S. Stocking & Associates (Eds.) *Protecting children from abuse and neglect* (pp. 94–108). CA: Jossey-Bass.

Garbarino, J. & Sherman, D. (1980). High-risk neighborhoods and high- risk families: The human ecology of child maltreatment. *Child Development, 51,* 188–198.

Gaster, S. (1991). Urban children's access to their neighborhood. *Environment and Behavior, 23*(1), 70–85.

Gaudin, J., Polansky, N., Kilpatrick, A., & Shilton, P. (1993). Loneliness, depression, stress, and social support in neglectful families. *American Journal of Orthopsychiatry, 63*(4), 597–605.

Gaudin, J., & Pollane, L. (1983). Social networks, stress and child abuse. *Children and Youth Services Review, 5,* 91–102.

Gelles, R. (1992). Poverty and violence toward children. *American Behavioral Scientist, 35*(3), 258–274.

Gephart, M. (1997). Neighborhoods and communities as contexts for development. In J. Brooks-Gunn, G. Duncan, & L. Aber (Eds.), *Neighborhood poverty: Context and consequences for children* (pp. 1– 43). New York: Russell Sage.

Gephart, M. (1989). Neighborhoods and communities in concentrated poverty. *Items, 43*(4), 84–92.

Gerson, K., Steuve, C., Fisher, C. (1977). Attachment to place. In E. F. Fischer et al. (Eds.). *Networks and places* (pp. 139–161). New York: Free Press.

Glynn, T. (1981). Psychological sense of community: Measurement and application. *Human Relations, 34,* 780–818.

Gordon, M., Riger, S., Lebailly, R., & Heath, L. (1980). Crime, women and the quality of urban life. *Signs, 5,* 144–160.

Gordon, R., Chase-Lansdale, L., Matjasko, J., & Brooks-Gunn, J. (1997). Young mothers living with grandmothers and living apart: How neighborhood and household contexts relate to multigenerational coresidence in African American families. *Applied Developmental Science, 1*(2), 89–106.

Hashima, P., & Amato, P. (1994). Poverty, social support, and parental behavior. *Child Development, 65,* 394–403.

Hogan, D., & Kitagawa, E. (1985). The impact of social status, family structure, and neighborhood on the fertility of black adolescents. *American Journal of Sociology, 90,* 825–852.

Horowitz, F.D. (Ed.). (1989). Children and their development: Knowledge base, research agenda, and social policy application [special issue]. *American Psychologist, 44*(2).

Hoyle, R. (1995). The structural equation modeling approach. In R. Hoyle (Ed.), *Structural equation modeling* (pp. 1–15). Thousand Oaks, CA: Sage.

Hoyle, R., & Panter, A. (1995). Writing about structural equation models. In R. Hoyle (Ed.), *Structural equation modeling* (pp. 158–176). Thousand Oaks, CA: Sage.

Hu, L., & Bentler, P. (1995). Evaluating model fit. In R. Hoyle (Ed.), *Structural equation modeling* (pp. 76–99). Thousand Oaks, CA: Sage.

Huckfeldt, R. (1983). Social contexts, social networks and urban neighborhoods: Environmental constraints on friendship choice. *American Journal of Sociology, 89*, 651–669.

Hutcheson, J., Black, M., Talley, M., Dubowitz, H., Berenson-Howard, J., Starr, R. & Thompson, B. (1997). Risk-status and home intervention among children with failure-to-thrive: Follow-up at age four. *Journal of Pediatric Psychology, 22*, 651–669.

Huston, A., Garcia-Coll, C., & McLoyd, V. (Eds.). (1994). Special issue on children and poverty. *Child Development, 65*, 275–282.

Janowitz, M. (1978). *The last half-century: Societal change and pol itics in America.* Chicago: The University of Chicago Press.

Jargowski, P., & Bane, M. (1991). Ghetto poverty in the United States, 1970–1980. In J. C. Jencks & P. Peterson (Eds.), *The urban underclass* (pp. 235– 273). Washington, DC: The Brookings Institution.

Jarrett, R. (1995). Growing-up poor: The family experiences of socially mobile youth in low income African American neighborhoods. *Journal of Adolescent Research, 10*(1), 111–135.

Jencks, C. & Mayer, S. (1990). The social consequences of growing-up in a poor neighborhood. In L. Lynn & M. McGeary (Eds.), *Inner-city poverty in the United States* (pp. 111–186). Washington, DC: National Academy Press.

Jencks, C., & Mayer, S. (1990). Residential segregation, job proximity, and black job opportunities. In L. Lynn & M. McGeary

(Eds.), *Inner-city poverty in the United States* (187–222). Washington, DC : National Academy Press.

Jencks , C., & Peterson, P. (Eds.), *The urban underclass*. Washington, DC: The Brookings Institution.

Jennings, K., Stagg, V., & Connors, R. (1991). Social networks and mothers' interactions with their preschool children. *Child Development, 62*, 966– 978.

Jöreskog, K. & Sörbom, D. (1992). LISREL VIII: A guide to the program and applications. Mooresville, IN: Scientific Software.

Kasarda, J., & Janowitz, M. (1974). Community attachment in mass society. *American Sociological Review, 39*, 328–339.

Korbin, J. & Coulton, C. (1997). Understanding the neighborhood context for children and families: Combining epidemiological and ethnographic approaches. In J. Brooks-Gunn, G. Duncan, & L. Aber (Eds.), *Neighborhood poverty: Context and consequences for children* (pp. 65–79). New York, NY: Russell Sage.

Korte, C. (1983). Help seeking in a city: Personal and organizational sources of help. In A. Nadler, J. Fisher & B. De Paulo (Eds.), *New directions in helping* (Vol. 3 Applied perspectives on help-seeking and receiving) (pp. 255– 271). New York: Academic Press.

Kromkowski, J. (1976). Neighborhood deterioration and juvenile crime. Washington, DC: National Technical Information Service (No. PB-260 473), US Department of Commerce, August 1976.

Kupersmidt, J., Griesler, P., De Rosier, M., Patterson, C., & Davies, P. (1995). Childhood aggression and peer relations in the context of family and neighborhood factors. *Child Development, 66*, 360–375.

Lawton, M., Nahemov, L., & Yeh, T. (1980). Neighborhood environment and the well-being of older tenants in planned housing. *International Journal of Aging and Human Development, 11*, 211–227.

Lempers, J., Clark-Lempers, D., & Simmons, R. (1989). Economic hardship, parenting, and distress in adolescence. *Child Development, 60*, 25–49.

Levitt, M., Weber, R., & Clark, M. (1986). Social network relationships as sources of maternal support and well-being. *Developmental Psychology, 22,* 310–316.

Lewis, D., & Maxfield, M. (1980). Fear in the neighborhoods: An investigation of the impact of crime. *Journal of Research on Crime and Delinquency, 17,* 160–189.

Liska, A., Sanchirico, A., & Reed, M. (1988). Fear of crime and con strained behavior: Estimating a reciprocal effects model. *Social Forces, 66,* 827–837.

Logan, J., & Spitze, G. (1994). Family neighbors. *American Journal of Sociology, 100*(2), 453–476.

Lynch, M., & Cicchetti, D. (1998). An ecological transactional analysis of children and contexts: The longitudinal interplay among child maltreatment, community violence, and children's symptomatology. *Development and Psychopathology, 10,* 235–267.

Lynn, L., & McGeary, M. (1990). *Inner-city poverty in the United States.* Washington, D.C.: National Academy Press.

MacCallum, R. (1995). Model specification. In R. Hoyle (Ed.), *Structural equation modeling* (pp. 16–36). Thousand Oaks, CA: Sage.

Mann, P. (1970). The Neighborhood. In R. Gutman & D. Popenoe (Eds.), *Neighborhood, city and metropolis.* New York: Random House.

Martin, E., & Martin, J. (1978). *The black extended family.* Chicago: University of Chicago Press.

Massey, D., & Denton, N. (1989). Hypersegregation in U.S. metro politan areas: Black and Hispanic segregation along five dimensions. *Demography, 26*(3), 373–393.

Massey, D., & Hajnal, Z. (1995). The changing geographic structure of black-white segregation in the United States. *Social Science Quarterly, 76*(3), 527–542.

Mayer, S., & Jencks, C. (1990). Growing-up in poor neighborhoods: How much does it matter? *Science, 243,* 1441–1446.

McLanahan, S., & Booth, K. (1991). Mother-only families: Problems, prospects, and politics. In A. Booth (Ed.), *Contemporary families: Looking forward, looking back* (pp.405–428). Minneapolis, MN: National Council on Family Relations.

McLanahan, S., & Garfinkel, I. (1993). Single mothers, the underclass and social policy. In W. J. Wilson, (Ed.), *The ghetto underclass* (109–121). Newbury Park, CA: Sage.

McLeod, J., & Shanahan, M. (1996). Trajectories of poverty and children's mental health. *Journal of Health and Social Behavior*, 37, 207–220.

McLeod, J., & Shanahan, M. (1993). Poverty, parenting and children's mental health. *American Sociological Review*, 58, 351–366.

McLoyd, V. (1998). Socioeconomic disadvantage and child development. *American Psychologist*, 53(2), 185–204.

McLoyd, V., & Wilson, L. (1991). The strain of living poor: Parenting, social support, and child mental health. In A. Huston (Ed.), *Children in Poverty: Child development and public policy* (pp. 105–135). New York: Cambridge University Press.

McMillan, D., & Chavis, D. (1986). Sense of community: A definition and theory. *Journal of Community Psychology*, 14, 6–23.

Mierly, M., & Baker, S. (1983). Fatal house fires in an urban population. *Journal of the American Medical Association*, 249, 1466–1468.

Morris, P., & Hess, K. (1975). *Neighborhood power: The new localism*. Boston: Beacon Press.

Mrazek, P. & Haggerty, R. (Eds.). (1994). *Reducing risks for mental disorders*. Washington, DC: National Academy Press.

O'Campo, P., Xue, X., Wang, M., & O'Brien, M. (1997). Neighborhood risk factors for low birthweight in Baltimore: A multilevel analysis. *American Journal of Public Health*, 87(4), 597–603.

Pandey, S. & Coulton, C. (1994). Unraveling neighborhood change using two-wave panel analysis: A case study of Cleveland in the 1980s. *Social Work Research*, 18(2), 83–96.

Patterson, C., Kupersmidt, J., & Vaden, N. (1990). Income level, gender, ethnicity, and household composition as predictors of children's school based competence. *Child Development*, 61, 485–494.

Pelton, L. (1989). *For reasons of poverty: A critical analysis of the public child welfare system in the U.S.A.* New York: Praeger.

Pelton, L. (1994). The role of material factors in child abuse and neglect. In G. Melton & F. Barry (Eds.), *Protecting children from abuse and neglect* (pp. 131–181). New York: The Guilford Press.

Perkins, D., Meeks, J., & Taylor, R. (1992). The physical environment of street blocks and residents' perceptions of crime and disorder: Implications for theory and measurement. *Journal of Environmental Psychology, 12*, 21–34.

Perkins, D., Florin, P., Rich, R., Wandersman, A., & Chavis, D. (1990). Participation and the social and physical environment of residential blocks: Crime and community context. *American Journal of Community Psychology, 18*(1), 83–114.

Polansky, N., Gaudin, J., Ammons, P., & Davies, K. (1985). The psychological ecology of the neglectful mother. *Child Abuse and Neglect, 9*, 265–275.

Pratt, M., Kerig, P., Cowan, P., & Cowan, C. (1988). Mothers and fathers teaching 3-year-olds: Authorative parenting and adult scaffolding of children's learning. *Developmental Psychology, 24*, 832–839.

Riger, S. & Lavrakas, P. (1981). Community ties: Patterns of attachment and social interaction in urban neighborhoods. *American Journal of Community Psychology, 9*(1), 55–66.

Ringel, N. & Finkelstein, J. (1991). Differentiating neighborhood satisfaction and neighborhood attachment among urban residents. *Basic and Applied Social Psychology, 12*(2), 177–193.

Roberts, E. (1997). Neighborhood social environments and the distribution of low birthweight in Chicago. *American Journal of Public Health, 87*(4), 597–603.

Robins, L. N., Helzer, J. E., Croughan, J., & Ratcliff, K. S. (1981). National Institute of Mental Health Diagnostic Interview Schedule: Its history, characteristics, and validity. *Archives of General Psychiatry, 38*, 381–389.

Sameroff, A. & Seifer, R. (1995). Accumulation of environmental risk and child mental health. In H. Fitzgerald, B. Lester, & B. Zuckerman (Eds.), *Children of poverty* (pp. 233–254). New York: Garland Publishing, Inc.

Sampson, R. (1987). Urban black violence: The effects of joblessness and family disruption. *American Journal of Sociology, 93,* 348–382.

Sampson, R. (1991). Linking the micro- and the macrolevel dimensions of community social organization. *Social Forces, 70*(1), 43–64.

Sampson, R. (1992). Family management and child development: Insights from social disorganization theory. In J. McCord (Ed.), *Advances in criminological theory,* Volume 2, (pp. 63–93), New Brunswick, NJ:Transaction Publishers.

Sampson, R. (1993). The community context of violent crime. In W. J. Wilson (Ed.), *Sociology and the public agenda* (pp. 259–286). Newbury Park, CA: Sage.

Sampson, R. & Groves, W. (1989). Community structure and crime: Testing social disorganization theory. *American Journal of Sociology, 94,* 775– 802.

Sampson, R. & Laub, H. (1994). Urban poverty and the family context of delinquency: A new look at structure and process in a classic study. *Child Development, 65,* 523–540.

Sandler, I. (1985). Children's environments and mental health: Opportunity and responsibility. *American Journal of Community Psychology, 13*(4), 335–337.

Sarason, S. (1974). *The psychological sense of community: Prospects for a community psychology.* San Francisco, CA: Jossey Bass.

Sarri, R. (1988). The impact of federal policy change on the well-being of poor women and children. In P. Voydonoff & L. Majka (Eds.), *Families and economic distress* (pp. 209–232). Newbury Park, CA: Sage.

Schorr, L. (1988). *Within our reach: Breaking the cycle of disadvantage.* New York: Doubleday.

Schubiner, H., Scott, R., & Tzelepis, A. (1993). Exposure to violence among inner-city youth. *Journal of Adolescent Health, 14*(3), 214–219.

Schumacker, R. & Lomax, R. (1996). *A Beginner's Guide to Structural Equation Modeling.* Mahwah, NJ: Erlbaum.

Seagull, E. (1987). Social support and child maltreatment: A review of the evidence. *Child Abuse and Neglect, 11,* 41–52.

Skogan, W. (1990). *Disorder and decline: Crime and the spiral of decay in American neighborhoods.* New York: Free Press.

Smeeding, T. & Rainwater, L. (1995). Cross-national trends in income poverty and dependence: The evidence for young adults in the eighties. In K. McFate (Ed.), *Poverty, inequality, and the future of social policy.* New York: Russell Sage Foundation.

Smith, D., & Jarjoura, G. (1988). Social structure and criminal victimization. *Journal of Research on Crime and Delinquency, 25,* 27–52.

Spencer, M. (1990). Development of minority children: An introduction. *Child Development, 61*(1), 267–269.

Stack, C. (1974). *All our kin.* New York: Harper.

Stafford, M., & Galle, O. (1984). Victimization rates, exposure to risk, and fear of crime. *Criminology, 22,* 173–185.

Taylor, R. (1986). Receipt of support from family among Black Americans: Demographic and familial differences. *Journal of Marriage and the Family, 48,* 67–77.

Taylor, R. (1997). Social order and disorder of street blocks and neighborhoods: Ecology, microecology, and the systemic model of social disorganization. *Journal of Research in Crime and Delinquency, 34*(1), 114–155.

Taylor, R. (1995). The impact of crime on communities. *Annals of the American Academy of PSS, 539,* 28–45.

Taylor, R. & Covington, J. (1993). Community structural change and fear of crime. *Social Problems, 40*(3), 374–395.

Taylor, R., Gottfredson, S., & Brower, S. (1985). Attachment to place: Discriminant validity, and impact of disorder and diversity. *American Journal of Community Psychology, 13*(5), 525–542.

Thorndike, R., Hagen, E., & Sattler, J. (1986). *The Stanford-Binet, Fourth Edition.* Chicago, IL: Riverside.

Thomson, E., Hanson, T., & McLanahan, S. (1994). Family structure and child well-being: Economic resources vs. parental resources. *Social Forces, 73,* 221–242.

Tienda, M. (1991). Poor people and poor places: Deciphering neighborhood effects on poverty outcomes. In J. Huber (Ed.) *Macro-linkages in sociology* (pp. 244–262). Newbury Park, CA: Sage Publication.

Tracy, E. (1990). Identifying social support resources of at-risk families. *Social Work, 35,* 252–258.

Ullman, J. (1996). Structural equation modeling. In B. Tabachnick & L. Fidell (Eds.), *Using multivariate statistics* (pp. 709–811). New York: Harper Collins.

Unger, D., & Wandersman, A. (1982). Neighboring in an urban environment. *American Journal of Community Psychology, 10*(5), 493–509.

Unger, D., & Wandersman, A. (1985). The importance of neighbors: The social, cognitive, and affective components of neighboring. *American Journal of Community Psychology, 13*(2), 139–169.

U.S. Bureau of the Census (1992). *Poverty in the United States: 1991.* (Current Population reports, Series P-60, No. 181). Washington, DC: U.S. Government Printing Office.

Wacquant, L., & Wilson, W. J. (1993). The cost of racial and class exclusion in the inner city. In W. J. Wilson, (Ed.), *The ghetto underclass* (pp. 25– 42). Newbury Park, CA: Sage.

Walker, K. & Furstenberg, F. (1994, August). *Neighborhood settings and parenting strategies.* Paper presented at the annual meeting of the American Sociological Association, Los Angeles, California.

Warren, D. (1980). Support systems in different types of neighborhoods. In J. Garbarino, S. Stocking, & Associates (Eds.), *Protecting children from abuse and neglect* (pp. 61–93). CA: Jossey-Bass.

Weenig, M., Schmidt, T., & Midden, C. (1990). Social dimensions of neighborhoods and the effectiveness of information programs. *Environment and Behavior, 22,*(1), 27–54.

Werner, C. (1987). A transactional approach to neighborhood social relationships. In S. Oskamp & S. Spacapan (Eds.), *Interpersonal processes* (pp. 25–57). Newbury Park, CA: Sage.

West, J., & Brick, J. (1991). *The national household education survey: A look at young children at risk.* Paper presented at the annual meeting of the American Statistical Association, Atlanta, GA.

West, S., Finch, J., & Curran, P. (1995). Structural equation models with nonnormal variables. In R. Hoyle (Ed.), *Structural equation modeling* (pp. 56–75). Thousand Oaks, CA: Sage.

White, M. (1987). *American neighborhoods and residential differentiation*. New York: Russell Sage Foundation.

White, M., Kasl, S., Zahner, G., & Will, J. (1987). Perceived crime in the neighborhood and mental health of women and children. *Environment and Behavior, 19*(5), 588–613.

Wilson, W. (1991). Studying inner-city social dislocations: The challenge of public agenda research. *American Sociological Review, 56*, 1–14.

Wilson, W. J. (1993). The underclass: Issues, perspectives and public olicy. In W. J. Wilson, (Ed.), *The ghetto underclass* (pp. 1–24). Newbury Park, CA: Sage.

Wilson, W. (1994). *Crisis and challenge: Race and the new urban poverty*. The 1994 Ryerson Lecture, University of Chicago.

Wilson, W. J. (1996). Jobless ghettos and the social outcome of youngsters. In P. Moen, G. Elder, & K. Luscher (Eds.), *Examining lives in context* (pp. 527–543). Washington, DC: American Psychological Association.

Zill, N., Moore, K., Smith, E., Stief, T., & Coiro, M. (1995). The life circumstances and development of children in welfare families: A profile based on national survey data. In P. L. Chase-Lansdale & J. Brooks-Gunn (Eds.), *Escape from poverty* (pp. 38–59). New York: Cambridge University Press.

Zuravin, S. (1986). Residential density and urban child maltreatment: An aggregate analysis. *Journal of Family Violence, 1*(4), 307–322.

Zuravin, S. (1989). The ecology of child abuse and neglect: Review of the literature and presentation of the data. *Violence and Victims, 4*, 101–120.

Index